Dear Mum and Dad

ISBN 978-1-84999-519-3

For more information about Terry Wheeler and his books, see his web site at **www.terrywheeler.net**

Dear Mum and Dad

Letters from Provence

TERRY WHEELER

for Anne
  — Best wishes,
     Terry Wheeler
          02.04.2008   3

ACKNOWLEDGEMENTS

I would like to thank Hugh who loaned us his caravan and whose generous action started this story some twenty-six years ago.

I would like to thank all those people who have unwittingly contributed to this book because they were there when I was people-watching. I am truly grateful to them for the hours of enjoyment they have given me and if I have seemed a little harsh in their depiction I apologise. I extend my special thanks to all the good people of Villes sur Auzon who made us so welcome when we were visiting and then living there; I remember them all with the greatest respect.

I would like to thank my editor Elizabeth Hauke of Rivendell Communications, who rescued my ramblings from near incoherence and tidied them into their present form. The picture on the back cover was given to me by Rebecca Zingel and I thank her for it.

Finally, I would like to thank my wife with whom I have shared every event on these pages and who has sat by patiently while I scribbled my notes, took my pictures and apparently stared into space. Our children accompanied us throughout the early chapters, visited us through the central portion of the book and are now bringing their own families to visit us. I thank them for giving me a reason to explore France.

Terry Wheeler spent his working life as a teacher in West Sussex. Taking advantage of the long summer holidays he and his family began to travel in France, towing their caravan and visiting new regions each year. Finally, he and his wife bought a little holiday home in Provence and four years later they retired there to live. He still lives in France, although he is often in England to visit his family or to give talks. Terry regularly gives talks based on this book – for more information see his website – www.terrywheeler.net

He has been writing for the last eight years and has already published *Eric the First* which is a humorous account of a year in Eric's life as he turns into a teenager.

Contents

Even now I can remember the first glimpse we had of the Vaucluse Plateau and Mont Ventoux. With the scents of lavender, thyme, rosemary and pine in our nostrils we drove south through a little pine forest and then the plateau spread out in front of us, dominated by the mountain. There are moments in our lives which, when seen with the benefit of hindsight, prove to have been pivotal and this was one of them, although at the time we were blissfully unaware of it. The spell was almost wrought and we set out on the path from which there would be no deviation.

Villes Sur Auzon

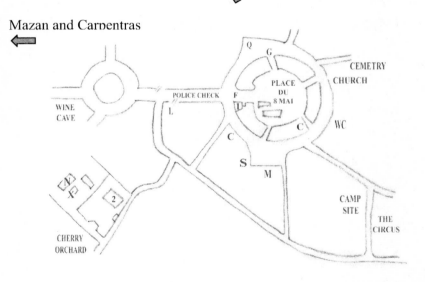

Mont Ventoux

Mazan and Carpentras

Gorges De La Nesque

1	Our First House	Q	Quiet Thoughts
2	Our New House	L	The Village Lavabo
M	The Mairie	G	The Grand Portail
N	Our Neighbours' House	C	The Cafés
X	Our Neighbours' Lavabo	S	The Village School
F	The Fountain		

1

A matchless experience

It was the end of January 1982, and our fourth child had just been born. Our lives were busy, we were desperately short of free time and the winter was beginning to drag as only a cold, dull and wet English winter can. We needed to break the mould. As luck would have it, a bundle of magazines arrived through the post for Christine, my wife. By another quirk of fate I was looking through them one evening, waiting for her to come down from settling the baby, and amongst them there was a magazine advertising family camping holidays in Europe. It was to change our lives although I didn't appreciate its full significance at the time, and the moment passed almost un-noticed.

The idea lay dormant for a while but as the seemingly endless winter dragged on, it re-surfaced. The thought of camping utterly appalled me but the pictures of sandy beaches and rolling green hills, of chateaux and vineyards attracted me. We usually managed a week's bed and breakfast in one of the more rural parts of England but, now that we had four girls, it was beginning to become too expensive. All the more so when I compared it with the price of camping holidays abroad.

We were desperate and even considered buying a tent to give life under canvas a try. Our evenings were filled with discussions as we tried to evaluate the pros and cons of camping and then Christine had an idea. Why didn't we ask her father if we could borrow his caravan? The long and the short of it was that we did, he was willing, we had the car adapted for towing and we awaited the arrival of the caravan with great excitement.

I should tell you that I had never towed a caravan, or taken a holiday in one, and so it was potentially quite a rash step to take a caravan abroad for two weeks in France. But driven by necessity, as well as curiosity, we had made the reckless decision to borrow the caravan and now we were set for France. This is the account of our first expedition.

Sussex
14th July 1982

Dear Mum and Dad,

I hope you have recovered from the shock of hearing that we are proposing to take the children caravanning in France this summer. We have been busy doing our research and have read every book about caravans that we have been able to borrow from our local library and also some about the various regions of France.

Our friends are convinced that we are mad. To be honest, they have always suspected this and our determination to take three children and a new-born baby to France has done nothing but confirm their worst fears. If we are to believe what we read, they are probably correct; but we need a holiday so desperately that we have decided to ignore most of the 'good' advice which we have been so freely given as well as that which we have laboriously researched.

How could we be so uncaring as to take a young baby to France, our friends ask us. Did they not know, we ask ourselves, that babies are not only being born in France but that they seem to flourish? You will need to take tinned butter and powdered milk the books inform us; and tinned

12

meat, tinned fruit and water to drink … the list is endless. How is it, we wonder, that the French seem to survive on their own local food? The books labour the point of telling us that the French have 'peculiar' eating habits. But what about fresh-baked bread bought daily and still warm from the oven, or about Normandy butter and cheese, about fresh-caught fish sold from the boats on the beach or about fresh vegetables bought from a market stall … or at least, that is what our brochure promises us.

Christine's father brought the caravan up last weekend and we've had the car fitted for towing. Since I've never towed a caravan before it only seemed common sense to try out the 'rig' first and so we agreed to take the caravan on a trial run to make sure we could actually tow it and set it up. We selected a quiet mid-week afternoon for this initial outing and decided to drive through Petworth, a nearby town notorious for its difficult road system which has a number of narrow roads incorporating a series of right angled bends. If we came through unscathed, we reasoned, there would be nothing that we couldn't do.

We had already chosen the spot where we were going to have tea, just the other side of Petworth on a quiet stretch of deserted country road. It was a large lay by into which we could easily drive and which would not require us to turn round or to undertake any other tricky manoeuvres.

The hitching up was easy, we had practised that, and we sailed through our pre-drive checks, the girls standing behind and eagerly reporting as we tried left blinker, right blinker, flashers, brake lights, side lights … a routine we will doubtless be repeating countless times in years to come but which, on this occasion, was excitingly new. With everybody seated in the car and the huge wing mirrors adjusted we set off looking forward to the delights of tea in the country with just the birds and perhaps a ruminating cow or two for company.

Negotiating access to the road was difficult since our drive is long and tree-lined with overhanging branches, and there are a number of large pot holes as well as a bend half way along just to make things more interesting. The road, when we reached it, was narrow and our gate posts left little room for manoeuvring so, in order to turn out from them, we had to drive over the road into the entrance to the house opposite, taking care to miss the drainage ditch, and then make a sharp turn back on to the road. Fortunately at that time of day few vehicles used our road and we managed without any real mishaps. Once we were on the road we re-adjusted the wing mirrors which had been knocked out of alignment by the trees along our drive, and set off.

Progress on the open road was slow for a while since it took time to adjust to the way the car reacted to towing the extra weight, as well as the increased length, but by the time we had climbed a couple of hills, experienced the way the car took tight bends and worked out stopping distances we felt reasonably happy. Fortunately, since the car was high and the caravan windows were low, I had through vision and could check the car's rear view mirror as well as the wing mirrors, quite a bonus in deciding what the cars behind were about to do.

The buzz of the children's chatter died as we came into the next town; it was as if they knew that this was the time for crossed fingers and whispered prayers. In the event the traffic was moving so slowly through the congested little town that we had no problems either in keeping up or negotiating the bends. It was a valuable lesson; take your time and the problems disappear, rush and the problems multiply alarmingly. Back on the open road we sailed along on a cloud of euphoria and reached our lay-by, fortunately empty, with no further problems; the volume of the girl's chatter had regained its former happy level.

The next part of the routine was easy. Everybody knew what to do: they had been assigned tasks according to their age. Mummy would look after the baby, Elizabeth at the tender age of two was responsible for retrieving the winding handle for the corner steadies, Samantha, who was eleven, fetched the wood blocks for the corner steadies and Karen, since she was the eldest at thirteen, was ready to place the blocks as I wound down the corner braces, vitally important if the van was to be stable when we were all inside.

14

I ticked off the action plan in my head. Check the hand brake, disconnect the electrics and unhitch, wind down the braces, check the spirit level to make sure that the van is level, find a flat place for the step block and warn the girls to be careful since the door into the van is quite high off the ground - even with the steps, it's tricky to negotiate. The baby was blissfully asleep as the table was put up. The plates were found and the cups set ready - our new plates and cups bought especially for the caravan. We had a camping kettle - one of those with a screw cap on the spout - and I had pre-filled it to save the business of having to connect the water barrel and draw water from the tap. I went out to the front locker to turn on the gas.

Back inside Christine was searching through the drawers. For cutlery, I assumed, although I could see that the knives were already on the table and spoons were in the saucers.

'Don't forget to unscrew the cap from the kettle,' I needlessly reminded her.

I had visions of the kettle boiling with its screw-cap still in place and could too easily envisage the ensuing explosion. Her retort was characteristically swift and to the point and so I re-took my place on the bench with the girls and waited patiently as she continued to rifle through the drawers.

'It seems a little rocky,' I said, as another drawer was slammed and the silence became more intense. 'I think I'll check the corner steadies now it's had time to settle.'

I went outside and wound each corner brace down a further half turn and then came back in. The kettle was still on the stove and Christine was now looking through the clothes lockers. I was about to suggest that the kettle would probably boil more quickly if the gas was lit, when I was confronted by my obviously irate wife.

'What did you do with the matches?'

'I haven't got them. You packed the van.'

'Well, they're not here. You must have put them somewhere.'

'I haven't touched anything. They're where you put them.'

'Well I can't find them.'

'You did pack them?' I asked without thinking. It was not a wise question.

'If you think you can do better then why didn't you do it?'

No use my saying that it had been repeatedly stressed to me that the packing was not my job, that I had been told not to interfere and that if I intended to check everything ...

So there we were, half-past five on a balmy July afternoon, sitting round the table neatly set for tea, with the cake on the plates, the kettle on the stove and fresh air gently blowing through the open windows. The only sound was the gentle snoring of the sleeping baby. Stony silence ensued for several minutes and continued while we dryly munched our way through the cake.

Re-packing was accomplished in a short time, also in silence apart from some rather firm closing of drawers and lockers, and we re-hitched, still in silence. The only sounds over the next few minutes were the okay calls as we went through the pre-drive tests, and even they were subdued.

The final irony occurred when the van was re-parked in our drive and we had resumed conversation.

'I know I put them in,' Christine said. 'I put them in this drawer here, so that I'd know where they were.'

She opened the drawer and the box was exactly where she had put it. Confirmation, if ever we needed it, that we were ready for a holiday.

2

Our first attempt

Bléré Camp Site
Loire Valley, France
10th August 1982

Dear Mum & Dad,

I know you still think that we're mad so I thought I'd better write to reassure you that we have arrived in France and are actually enjoying our holiday.

It was a bit weird getting up in the dark and driving off into the unknown but we reached Dover in plenty of time. The roundabouts caused us a few scary moments as we approached the docks, but remembering Petworth, we took them slowly and everything went okay. We arrived at the docks two hours early but the man in the ticket office let us through and told us where to park; he said that there might be a spare place on an earlier ferry. In the event, we were ushered forward an hour earlier than our booking. We were a bit nervous about driving on to the ferry but the sea was quite calm and we'd watched others do it so I shut my eyes (not literally!) and followed the car in front.

Parking on the ferry was a bit tight but we managed to keep in line and we were up on deck within a couple of minutes. The girls and I watched as they lowered the safety doors and then untied the lines anchoring us to the jetty. The whole boat started to shudder as they powered up the engines and the funnels belched smelly black smoke. We edged out of Dover very carefully and as soon as we were clear of the docks the engines were boosted up to full power. The sea had been calm inside the protection of the harbour but as soon as we were outside the waves hit us and the boat started rolling. It was funny watching Elizabeth trying to walk; she put her foot down as the boat rolled but the deck wasn't there so she lurched along giggling like an inebriated old woman even though she is only two - or as she would say, nearly three.

As soon as the boat was moving and there wasn't anything much to look at we went below – note the cunning nautical term – for a cup of coffee. There were croissants in the cafeteria and so we each had one, just in case we didn't have time to stop for breakfast when we reached France. The ferry was crowded and there wasn't anywhere to sit. Lots of people were asleep, sprawled over two or three seats or in the gangways so we went back up on top. The sun was up now, but it looked a bit watery so we found some seats on the leeward side and watched as France grew from a smudge on the horizon to a low contour and then until we could see the beginnings of buildings.

The crossing didn't take long, and soon we were told to go back to our cars. Because we were almost the last ones on we were also among the last ones off. I was very anxious about driving on the right but the funny thing was that everybody else was doing it! In fact, apart from going round the roundabouts the wrong way it was all quite simple and we began to relax.

The next challenge was driving on to our first campsite. The map seemed clear enough and we decided to take the journey slowly, particularly since Rebecca needed feeding. We pulled off the road at the next lay-by which was huge. The toilets were clean and there was water for drinking although we didn't need it because we'd filled the barrel before we left. We made a cup of coffee and the girls had some biscuits and went to play on the swings while Christine fed Rebecca.

Back on the road we headed for our first town. I don't know whether we were disappointed or relieved because there was a ring road and we were spared driving through. The country side was quite uninteresting at first, lots of industrial sites, but as soon as we'd left Calais behind we were into open fields and rolling hills. We found it strange that there were no hedges. The fields just stopped at the road edge. I think Karen and Samantha were finding it a bit of a squash in the back. They didn't complain, but we stopped quite often to give them a chance to get out and stretch their legs.

We passed through lots of little villages. The houses didn't have front gardens - most of them opened on to the pavement. Except that it wasn't a pavement like we have in England, but a wide gravel area with room for cars to park and people to walk by. There were a lot more trees on the edges of the road too, so the pavements were often quite shady; there were seats for people to sit out and lots of flowers planted out in beds or boxes. It all looked very bright and cheerful. We wondered how long they'd have lasted in our village. One night, we guessed, before the local youths pulled them up.

Well, we made it to our first camp site although we couldn't find it at first. We saw the signs and followed them as they took us off the main road and through the back roads of the town. In the end we were totally lost so I pulled off the road and Christine went and asked a passer by if they could tell us where the campsite was. We felt really foolish because we had actually parked outside it!

We drove in and they were very patient in the reception office and we managed to pay without any problems. They told us we could set up anywhere we wanted because they weren't busy so we found a spot in the afternoon sun and had a drink before we struggled with the awning. It took us a while to level the caravan and then we found the slope meant that we had to pull the awning down more on one side which made it all look a bit drunk, but we managed it okay and put the groundsheet down. Karen and Samantha were quite nervous about sleeping out in the awning, but as we pointed out - it was only like sleeping in a tent. Rebecca seemed unimpressed by our achievement and mostly slept or fed, although she did start to take more notice as soon as Christine started to cook our evening meal.

We slept the sleep of the just and awoke with the birds the next morning. We didn't bother to pack the caravan too carefully because we knew we'd be taking it all out again in the evening. We journeyed on and found our next site without any problem and set up camp as if we'd been doing it for ever.

We are now at our third campsite, in Bléré, the one where we're going to stay. We were a bit anxious that there wouldn't be room for us because we hadn't been able to book our plot in advance. But there was plenty of room and we chose a spot by the river Cher so that we can sit and look out across to the fields on the opposite bank. There is a weir down-river to our left. The fish swim up to it in the evenings and we watch them jump for the flies. There are huge sunflowers in the field opposite us and they seem to watch us as they turn their heads to the sun.

Our pitch is at one edge of the campsite so it's nice and quiet, which is good for the baby who can sleep in peace. There's a shop just outside the campsite which sells everything we need so life is very calm and comfortable. There's even a glass of wine on the table as I'm writing this letter! We plan to visit a chateau tomorrow. There are plenty to choose from so if we get lost we're bound to find another one nearby.

How are the cats? I expect that you're both enjoying the peace and quiet now we're away. Make the most of it because I'm sure the girls will be full of it when we get back. They haven't stopped talking yet – you've been warned!

3

Time flies when you're having fun

And the years that followed? Time flies when you're having fun. Certainly they were years filled with memories, varied in experience and yet unified by the irresistible attraction of France.

Over and again we were drawn back for a day trip, for an autumn break and, of course, for our summer holidays and some years we made the crossing four times. We experienced calm weather, rain, thunder and lightning, and even a cyclone. We crossed the Channel on quiet days when there was scarcely a wave in sight, with the sun beating down and everyone seeking shade under the deck awnings; and on one memorable October day, when the sea was so violent that we were held at the exit ramp until the waves were in the right position to drive up a ramp that was oscillating wildly. According to the weather we picked our way across the deck, littered with prostrate bodies taking advantage of a little early sun or made our way round a party of Brownies on a day trip, all being violently sick as they struggled to climb up to the deck for fresh air. Some autumn evenings the ferry was like a ghost ship and we seemed to be the only passengers and yet in summer it was often so crowded that there was no room to sit down.

We explored the Loire Valley, the Atlantic coast, Brittany, the Mediterranean and camped in the middle of Paris. We walked the cliffs at

Douarnenez, surfed at Biarritz and drove into the Pyrenees. We climbed over the Midi and discovered its Roman heritage. We bought mustard in Dijon, ham in Bayonne, champagne in Rheims, Camembert in Normandy, brioche in the Vendée and wine wherever we stayed. We lazed on beaches while the children dug in the sand, and in the evening we cooked on our barbecue. We discovered the Beauce and its tiny villages scorched by the sun. We fell in love with Chartres, walked along river banks, sat outside cafés under shady trees and visited wine caves cut deep into the hillsides. The children rode the mechanical horses in fairgrounds and we watched the stalls making sucettes (those delicious sugar sweets). We bought crêpes dripping with chocolate and jam and drank cider bailed from a bucket, complete with bits of straw, and we took our ease in the grounds of a château in the Dordogne, drinking sangria while the chef cooked our meal.

But strong currents were at work beneath the surface and the die was cast, even though we were as yet unaware of it. The years were marked by a pattern, as dependable as the seasons. We returned from our holiday and immediately began to wish we had visited a different place. The photographs came back from processing and once more we were immersed in the sights and sensations of our holiday which spurred us on to think about the next year. We made tentative plans and then, sitting in front of a winter fire, we changed our minds. As spring came into sight we started making our bookings, finding that if we booked the ferry sufficiently far ahead it was possible to benefit from significant discounts. By now we knew that it would always be possible to find space at a camp site without booking, but we still chose and booked our main centres in advance - it was an essential part of the ritual.

The girls grew up. Some years their friends came with us, some years one or other stayed at home with a holiday job, but still we made our annual pilgrimage. The caravan changed, we became more adept and mastered the skills of making and breaking camp in all weathers - from *scorching sun to howling wind and pouring rain, often giving the performance to an appreciative audience of fellow campers.*

On one memorable occasion, with the awning in the slot along the roof of the caravan, I fainted in the heat beneath the heap of canvas and my inert body had to be dragged into the van. On another, the poles collapsed, banging Christine on the head. It was greeted with laughter and applause by our Dutch neighbours who seemed to think that we had come simply to entertain them. I hoped that their grasp of English was not adequate to enable them to understand the torrent of words my wife aimed in my direction.

The outcome was inevitable - it was only a matter of time. Those dangerous currents, fast flowing beneath the apparent calm of our lives, were becoming stronger and ever more evident, although their first manifestation was unremarkable.

One year, walking the familiar route to the boulangerie in 'our village' on the Atlantic coast, we passed an empty house marked 'For Sale'. In our minds we took possession and planned the restoration of the derelict garden. We imagined ourselves having breakfast on the shady terrace and dinner at a candle-lit table with the gracious doors open to the cool evening air. It was a new game and we played it with diligence.

'You know the door to the left? Well, we could put a bench along the wall ...' Christine later said on a dull November afternoon.

The really worrying thing was that I knew exactly what she was talking about – the house in 'our village'...

And then we came to Provence. We had no experience of the region and made our choice entirely on the basis of the camp sites listed in our guide, settling for a small site to the west of Nîmes. This was the beginning of the final phase. Infection had set in and was festering in our subconscious although we were still blissfully unaware of the lurking danger.

The camp site was pleasant, even if largely unremarkable, and the region was interesting, rich in Roman remains and all manner of historic buildings and locations. The time passed all too quickly and we returned home still slightly intoxicated with the luminous quality of the light and the volatile scent of hot pines. Plans were made to return the following summer and we decided to try the other side of the auto-route, looking for a site near Avignon, the choice of location being made as before with the assistance of our redoubtable camping guide.

There are moments in our lives which, when seen with the benefit of hindsight, prove to have been pivotal and this was one of them, although at the time we were blissfully unaware of it. The spell was almost wrought and we set out on the path from which there would be no deviation.

Even now I can remember the first glimpse we had of the Vaucluse Plateau and Mont Ventoux. With the scents of lavender, thyme, rosemary and pine in our nostrils we drove south through a little pine forest and then the plateau spread out in front of us, dominated by the mountain. Others before us had been similarly entranced.

"First, surprised. Surprised by the strange lightness of the air and the immensity of the spectacle, I remained immobile, as if struck by stupor." (Petrarch, 1336)

The holiday was fine although the campsite was not greatly to our taste, occupied as it was by elderly British couples who were more intent on meeting up with their friends than exploring or enjoying the region. Every time a caravan left they shifted round until they had built up a British enclave where they sat all day in the shade of their awnings fortified with bottles of wine.

Walking in and around the tiny village we found the Municipal Camp Site which, although way down in the ratings, looked airy, calm and friendly. Maybe it would have been better to stay there. The scenery surrounding the village was stunning and there were plenty of places to visit. By the end of our stay we had only gained a taster of what the region had to offer and so we decided to come back to the area the following year.

The next summer, in pursuit of a better camp site, we turned once more to our guide book and arranged a stay at a highly rated site in the next village. A long, hot, dusty drive was finished off by a blocked auto route and a diversion over minor roads which were better suited to yaks than a caravan. We arrived tired and frustrated. The site filled us with horror. It was dilapidated and none too clean. Vans were pushed here and there in the shade under the trees, the facilities were old and the toilet block gave warning of its location well before we actually saw it.

We drove round once and left. It was a measure of how strongly we felt that we even gave up our not inconsiderable deposit before driving on to Villes sur Auzon and the Municipal Camp Site where there was plenty of room. We chose a plot with a view of Mont Ventoux and space all round us.

Our stay was magical. We continued to explore the area, became intoxicated with the local wine, literally on more than one evening, and reached the point where we admitted to each other that we 'liked' the area very much.

Fate twists and turns our lives in the strangest ways and it had not yet finished with us. On our frequent trips to the next village we passed a large, empty house with a 'For Sale' sign and finally curiosity won over discretion and we looked at the notice boards in the local estate agent's office. Lo and behold, we found the house in the centre of Mr Faucon's display and, plucking up courage we went in and asked if we could look over the house. The agent was most co-operative and took us over the house on two occasions.

We returned to England full of plans and went back to France the following October, staying in a flat at a nearby vineyard, for another look. The state of repair of the house caused us concern. Its previous occupants had separated after a particularly acrimonious divorce and had removed all the doors and radiators as part of their settlement. Since there was also considerable damp, the house began to look less attractive

- all the more so since its owners were not prepared to significantly lower their asking price.

Once more we returned to England. Sadly, the house we had fallen in love with was not on the market for long – it was bought by a Belgian business man. But by now we had decided that we had outgrown the caravan and we began seriously looking at French property adverts. We found that property prices were much lower in the south of France than they were in West Sussex and if we made some adjustments we thought it might be worth considering buying a house in France. But we felt that we needed to get the feel of what they were like. It is one thing to look at an advert but it is an entirely different experience when you see a house with your own eyes and so we decided to visit some properties on our next visit.

4

A man of property

Olonzac & Villes sur Auzon
August 1996

Dear Mum and Dad,

We are here in the south-west and ready to explore the housing market. Well, actually we're not. So much has happened since we were in touch that I think I'd better start at the beginning. In fact, we almost never made it here at all, since a car pulled out in front of us five minutes after we left home. The driver appeared to be anxious to be on his way and not a little merry, judging by his steering. How we avoided skidding I'll never know but we managed to bring the car and caravan to a stop as he sped off on his erratic way.

We've come here to see if we can find a small house to use as a holiday home. We've read the magazines, done our research and have selected our agent. We've opted for an expatriate, retired English estate agent who seems to be confident that he can find us exactly what we want. When we telephoned him he assured us that properties in his region were as plentiful as they were cheap and he immediately sent us descriptions of six that sounded ideal. We felt that we couldn't have asked for a better service, and having spoken to him felt confident that he was 'our man'. We duly made an appointment to view suitable properties.

As soon as we had disembarked we began the drive down the auto-route through the centre of France making excellent progress eagerly anticipating the pleasures that lay ahead. And then the auto-route stopped. Finding ourselves suddenly on minor roads, we encountered a series of fierce bends. To our horror, these were only the prelude to several chains of hairpin bends running up and down hills, and then a switchback from Hell which somewhat slowed our progress and affected my peace of mind a great deal. In places, loose gravel and potholes alternated with deep ruts threatening to overturn the caravan. The road finally settled down as we approached the Mediterranean.

We drove round Béziers several times searching in vain for a signpost with our destination written on it. Eventually – on our third circuit – we found our way. We found Olonzac to be a small, attractive town, but the signs for the campsite led us out of the town and into the surrounding garrigue. Then the signs petered out and we had to ask the way. Eventually, we found the site which was accessed along what looked like someone's front drive, and which was littered with parked cars making it very difficult to drive the caravan through. We were a little concerned because the sign said that it was a Naturist Site! Later we found out that this referred to another site, further away.

The campsite was not large, the sun was beating down and the temperature was well over 30°C so we were anxious to find a plot with some shade. The owner - a little man with a serious scowl - was Dutch as were most of the other campers. We drove round and there was only one spot with shade that was free, but the campers on the next plot had taken it over to dry their washing and park their car. It seemed an age in the baking sun while they cleared the plot for us. The site was a bit 'rough' and the grass needed cutting. Clearly whoever was developing the site had started with good intentions but ran out of steam.

At last we were able to relax and the following day we made our way into Olonzac for our appointment with the agent. He had put aside the whole day for us, promising us lunch in a local town. Based upon the charming and avuncular French agent we had met the previous year, our expectations were high.

'Love is blind', so the adage goes, and we were too besotted with the idea of owning a French house to notice our infatuation. From the first sight of the elderly gentleman dressed in khaki drill and wearing leather sandals with neat brown socks, sporting a straw hat perched soberly on an elegant head and carrying a leather document folder tucked beneath his arm, we should have been thinking Graham Greene and been on our guard.

Our senses should have been alerted when he let us into another agent's office who, he said, allowed him to use one of the back rooms. We should have realised that something was not quite right when he showed us his 'book' with the same, still unsold, properties that he had sent us a few months ago and, yet again, we should have been suspicious when he informed us that we would only be able to view 'a few' properties since he could only spare the morning. We ought to have asked ourselves why these properties, if they were so 'highly desirable', had not been 'snapped up' before we arrived.

But infatuation is blind. We wanted to believe in him and it was a sign of our naivety that we were even grateful when he recommended a place where we could buy a 'very reasonable' lunch. His secretary met us outside, and the way he held her hand while talking about his wife should have caused us more concern and our dormant suspicions should have been on high alert when they both climbed into his car.

We set out trying to keep his car in sight as they sped off into the countryside. He drove at such a rate that we had no time to look at the scenery and were in constant danger of losing him. In retrospect we wondered if that was what he was trying to achieve. The properties were all in the centres of tiny villages, often reached through a maze of narrow, one-way streets. The first was empty and he showed us round, pointing out its major attractions. There was a roof terrace where we could eat our evening meals - provided we were prepared to eat standing up and in shifts since there was only just room for one person to stand there at a time.

We moved on briskly to the next house, still lived in by its owner - a very elderly and none too clean gentleman. The chief attractions of this two roomed property were its toilet - in the bedroom wardrobe cupboard - and its potential for expansion which turned out to be a shared garage some distance down the road that could possibly have an extension built on its roof. The third property had a garden - one of our requests had been for space to eat outside - but the garden was over the road, down a step and along a path. He had saved the only property that seemed to be potentially what we were looking for until last but he didn't have time to show it to us. Perhaps we could make another appointment for some time next week? We left having told him that we would think about what we had seen and would be in touch … I think we all knew that this would never happen.

On the way back to our caravan the car began to play up. It gave a couple of coughs and stopped. We freewheeled off the road and waited, not knowing what to do. After a while we were able to restart the car, and so we crossed our fingers and returned to our caravan. We decided to move back up to our site in Provence and made plans to leave the following day.

Lightning does strike twice in the same spot! Hitched up and under way the following day the car stopped once more just outside the next village and when it refused to re-start we were forced to contact a local garage who tried to effect a repair. We camped on the garage forecourt while the owner awaited delivery of spare parts. Finally it became apparent that the repair would have to be undertaken by a franchise garage, and so he towed us, car and caravan to our next destination - Villes sur Auzon. Back in Provence we finally began to relax. Our insurance provided a hire car and we started to enjoy ourselves after a very inauspicious start to the holiday.

By now we had come to the conclusion that we would have to think seriously about replacing the car. We talked about it over the following week and began to investigate the option of selling both our cars and the caravan and buying a car which would be more economic to run. We were very impressed with the diesel Peugeot that we had been loaned and even more impressed by the cheapness of diesel as opposed to leaded four-star. If we had a little house somewhere near the campsite and could benefit from cheaper fuel prices …

Finally back in possession of our own car we made our way once more to the office of our 'avuncular' estate agent, Mr Faucon, and discussed our ideas with him in a mixture of French and English. It transpired that the agency was run by his wife and he just worked part time for something to do. However, he was most helpful and seemed to understand what we were looking for and was prepared to show us sample properties in and around the area.

As we had done with the last agent, we agreed a day to go 'out and about' with him. Unlike the agent in Olonzac, Bruno Faucon didn't let us down and he drove us to about six nearby properties, all within our price bracket. They varied in style and condition as much as in location, and they all seemed to be possible options although they were not exactly what we were looking for.

The first, decorated with deep red velvet flock wallpaper had an internal balcony which overlooked the main room downstairs. When we were standing on what he called the 'viewing platform' Bruno hinted that the house had previously had a 'difficult' reputation and had been used by a number of 'ladies' … another was immaculate but the garden would have required maintenance that we would be unable to provide. Another property was right on the edge of a busy road and backed on to a builder's yard which had clouds of dust rising, even as we visited the house.

Finally we arrived back in Villes sur Auzon for the last property which, Bruno said, had been partially restored but had been empty for a while and needed some attention. The property met all our 'essential' requirements and it even had a large upstairs terrace to enable us to eat out thereby saving us the need for a garden which would be difficult to maintain in our absences; it also possessed a garage. It was an old house, one of the original village properties, secure because it was right in the centre of the village, quaint although in need of a good clean and some external repair. All in all, an ideal place for holidays and a good base to use later when we might want to look around for a full-time residence in the distant days of retirement.

We are going to do our sums tonight – it really does look as if this might be the one.

5

Le Maçon

Camp Site
Villes sur Auzon
August

Dear Mum and Dad,

We thought you might like an update. Having made the decision to go ahead with the purchase of the house in Villes sur Auzon we made arrangements to meet with Mr Faucon, the agent, at the house. He suggested bringing the owner, André Charbonneau, with him so that we could discuss any points that concerned us. We made our way from the campsite down into the village in the early afternoon and found them both waiting for us in an upstairs room. The estate agent was accompanied by one of his sons who had a reasonable command of English and could translate for us. Just as well in the event.

Emitting a noise some two octaves below the vulgar end of a tuba, and forcing it past the last centimetre of a rapidly decaying hand-rolled cigarette, Mr Charbonneau extended his none too clean hand to me in a gesture of greeting.

"Bonjour!" I managed in reply.

This wasn't quite the limit of my French but I was not absolutely certain what he had said and I didn't want to appear more stupid than I was. In any case, I felt not a little uncomfortable since I had to crane my neck up at an extreme angle to look him in the face. Mr Charbonneau dominated the small room and at something over six feet or perhaps I should say in the region of two metres, he towered above me.

Burnt the colour of mahogany, André Charbonneau was a tall, thin man, not unlike a child's quickly drawn cartoon. He was wearing a virulently patterned shirt and a very cement-stained pair of shorts, the whole natty ensemble being set off by grubby white socks and the equivalent of Doc Martin boots. He had come straight from the house he had been working on for the last week. We immediately recognised him - partly because of his hat, a battered blue linen cloche (the sort of hat that old ladies wear in England when they want to go out in the mid-day sun) - and partly because he was a once-seen never-forgotten person, a 'character'.

Earlier at his office, the agent had told us that the owner of the house was a maçon, a traditional Provençal craftsman, and we had come expecting to see an elderly gentleman, possibly with a sheaf of drawings under his arm, who would talk to us about traditions and folk-lore, and enrich us with stories of village life. We had not made the connection with this man who had spent the last week working balanced on the roof of a tall three storey house near the boulangerie, taking the tiles and then part of the walls from the top of this house and throwing them down into the back of a lorry far below. The whole process seemed a little precarious and the style of work a little 'radical'. From his lofty vantage point it had only taken him two days to recognise my wife and daughters and he had taken to greeting them with a cheery wave, when they came into the village every day for our bread.

The presence of the maçon, close up and in the flesh, was a bit of a surprise and we tried not to be put off. He was clearly the kind of craftsman who knew what to do and how to do it, and he was not frightened to get his hands dirty – as well as most of the rest of him! Despite having a few reservations about the vigour of his work-style, we felt encouraged because at least one other person in the village had judged him suitable for employment. We were a little worried about the questions we had prepared in advance for him - perhaps they would seem too trivial or too obvious. We desperately wanted to present a good image - sharp and knowledgeable buyers, not the sort of people to be taken advantage of.

We began to raise the points that concerned us. When I say we 'raised' the points that concerned us, I mean that we told the agent's son who then queried some of the words – his English was not that good – and then spoke very rapidly with his father who in turn spoke in a quiet voice, and even more rapidly, with the maçon. We wished that we could understand what passed between them because, more often than not, the maçon greeted each question with a broad smile.

There were a number of damp patches on the ceilings of the top storey rooms and there were also signs of past damp on the floor. In our innocence we felt that this indicated that the roof leaked.

'All Provençal roofs let in a little rain,' the maçon assured us. 'You see, it's the pan tiles, one this way and then one that way. When they are first put up they are very good, but the leaves gather on them and if the gullies become blocked, sometimes a little water can make its way past them. It's really nothing to worry about, all we need to do is just clear the roof off and it will be fine!'

'What about the tiles that are missing?' I asked.

'Oh, the wind moves one or two. It's nothing to worry about. We'll put them back when we clear the roof.'

It looked as if this was going to be an annual maintenance task and I wondered if there was a more permanent solution. Mr Faucon pointed out that the newly laid roof terrace, which had once been another bedroom, had a problem with the slope of the floor since it directed the water towards, rather than away from, the house. And, outside the garage, the grating that should have covered the ventilation to the cellar was also missing.

'It's just the local children,' Mr Charbonneau said, 'they must have kicked it off.'

But it was the back wall of the house which concerned us the most.

The window opening in the smallest bedroom seemed to have been literally knocked into the wall - there were jagged edges of stone, no sill, and gaps round the window frame - either that or there had been an explosion and the window had been 'fitted' to take advantage of the resultant blast hole. There was also a mighty crack in the outside stonework lower down, and the whole wall was in a poor state of repair - with bits and pieces of it already fallen to the ground below. The surface seemed to be coming away in too many places to allow us to be confident that the rest would stay there for much longer, and the herringbone stonework beneath was partially exposed. We didn't think the wall was structurally unsound, but it needed re-surfacing. We pointed out that the gutter was suspended in mid-air, so far away from the wall that only falling raindrops had a chance of hitting it and certainly none of the roof water could reach it.

The maçon took pains to remind us that the house had recently been re-wired, and that there would be no problems with the plumbing. We went on to discuss the window over kitchen sink, which was so high up that Christine could not even reach it, let alone see through it, even if it had been glazed with clear glass. He agreed to replace it with a wider window, double-glazed with clear glass, and to make it lower so that we could see the view of the village square through it. He would also fit a security grill on the outside, very important for the insurance company and equally vital for our peace of mind when we were back in England.

Messrs Faucon and Charbonneau went into conference. We could just about pick out what the agent said but the assortment of guttural noises emitted by the maçon proved to be largely incomprehensible. Visions of unscrupulous agents flashed past my eyes and pictures of crafty Frenchmen taking advantage of gullible English tourists occupied my thoughts, aided no doubt by the twinkle in the maçon's eye and the permanent smile playing on his lips. However, we felt confident that the agent was fair - after all, he and his wife had taken great pains to help us, far beyond the call of duty or good business - and in some way we felt that he was on our side.

The upshot of this increasingly noisy conversation was that Mr Charbonneau produced a figure for the work that we wanted done and, since this was below our overall limit, we were about to agree to the deal when Mr Faucon went into conference with him again. Perhaps he thought we still looked worried. Certainly he seemed to be fighting our corner and he eventually persuaded the maçon to reduce the house price, splitting the cost of the alterations between us. The agent seemed to think this was an excellent arrangement and, since we could see no problem, we readily agreed and shook hands all round. The twinkle in the maçon's blue eyes still gave us a twinge of anxiety, but we instinctively liked him - only the future would tell us if he was a rogue.

Certainly we will look at this strange, tall, thin, brown-burnt man differently in future. As the maçon left to return to his work, the cigarette butt, which had long since gone out, was still fastened to his lip and we took the gurgle of sub-bass sounds he emitted as a farewell greeting and wished him 'au revoir.'

6

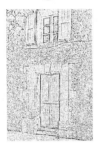

A new rhythm

We completed the purchase the following November on the day of Christine's fortieth birthday. We soon settled into the village and our coming and going life-style. The very first time we drew up the car outside our little house and began to unload our possessions, complete strangers stopped and chatted to us. The warmth of their welcome was genuine and we began to share their pride in this little place.

We had a lot of work to do on the house because, although it was essentially in good repair, it had few amenities. We cleaned, bought furniture, decorated, built a fire place and fitted a kitchen, drank the local wine and ate the local food. We felt we had a slice of heaven.

The following summer was our first long stay and we used the newly opened Channel Tunnel. We were greatly impressed by its speed and efficiency.

Le Cours
Villes sur Auzon
July 1997

Dear Mum and Dad,

We arrived with no mishaps, for a change. The journey started well until we met up with a group of elderly motorists who seemed to have no ambition to drive above 30mph. We had no chance of overtaking them and arrived at Folkestone five minutes too late to board our train. There were no problems, though, since they just put us in line for the next one. There were five men in the car parked in front of us and they grew more and more impatient. At first they confined their activity to getting in and out of the car and walking round it. When this palled they opened the boot and started on the packs of beer with which it was packed. This seemed a little like taking coal to Newcastle, since beer is so cheap in France. We were pleased to note that the driver drank Coca-cola. They were almost into their third round when we moved on and boarded the train. We were glad that they were merrily installed in the carriage in front of us!

The safety checks seemed to be taking an age and the compartment was getting very hot, even with the windows open and the fans running. The men in the compartment in front of us refreshed themselves with another beer. Eventually the announcer came on and apologised for the delay. The driver, he informed us, had been taken ill and a replacement driver was being brought in. We could see the men in the next compartment were not impressed by this news, and did the only thing they could in the circumstances – they had another round of beer.

An hour later – the time passed easily since we were entertained by the now very merry men in front of us – and the announcer came on yet again to tell us that they had been unable to replace the driver and we would be transferred to another train. Ten minutes later we were off-loaded and drove round the terminal again ...

We eventually arrived in France, disembarked and drove on until just after midnight. We were on the auto-route so we pulled into one of the stopping places and dozed until the morning light woke us up. The weather was cloudy and there was a little rain as we drove through Lyons but the weather gradually improved as we made our way south. Soon the cicadas were singing and the scent of the pine trees took over - we knew we were nearly there.

The house was much as we'd left it and, even though it was hot outside, the stone walls had kept it at about 24°C. We unpacked the car and spent most of the rest of the day snoozing, although we did stir our stumps to do some essential shopping for food in order to replenish our rapidly diminishing stock.

We had our evening meal up on the roof terrace and it was very pleasant in the warm evening breeze. The swallows were out again.

They've been here every evening, and circle in the sky above the terrace. I don't know if they do it just because they can or if they are gliding in the air currents and feeding on insects. They are a magnificent sight. There seems to be a squadron leader who is more daring than the rest. He flies at great speed and heads into the middle of them, daring any of them to get in his way. The 'Icarus swallows' seem to fly as high as they can until they become tiny dots just before they vanish. Then there are the 'Sergeant-Major' swallows, they sit on the side lines and twitter at the rest. I like to imagine that they are giving orders – right wheel, left turn, fast forward, dive – and the squad just follows their instructions. It's like a circus with clowns driving round in a crazy car and just before impact the leader tips a wing and wheels away, followed by the rest of his kamikaze crew.

Every evening seems to be marked by a general exodus of people from their houses. The young married couples push their offspring round the village in their buggies, stopping at the café for light refreshment.

They are followed by the more affluent who are on their 'fitness walk' and steam round the village a couple of times before collapsing at the café where they consume enough calories to replace those that they have so energetically walked off. The elderly might stroll a while, or they might just sit. They bring their chairs out on to the pavement and share the latest gossip with their neighbours over a glass or two of the local red stuff.

As soon as the swallows have roosted for the night and the more mature have gone in, the nocturnal species appear. Creeping along the alley ways, sneaking through doors and trying to remain invisible in the last rays of the sinking sun, the local youth come out. Because our house is at the entrance to the square and because we have a tree for shade and a seat for comfort, the space outside our house seems to be their favourite meeting place, day and night. This causes us no problem apart from the fact that some of them do not sleep at night; presumably they spend the daylight hours entombed in their beds. As soon as it's dark one or other of them arrives in a car and immediately pumps up the volume of the car stereo. After noisy greetings, much hugging and a great deal of kissing, they start on the pizza slices they have bought from down the road.

Shortly after midnight the next shift arrives on motor bikes – not the roaring monsters that pass us in a flash on the auto-route but the annoying little ones that buzz like angry wasps. They race round the village – no doubt driving a 'roaring monster' in their imagination – and then down the road, round the roundabout and back again. When they become tired of this they play football in the middle of the road. You can't really blame them for wanting to be up and about, the evenings are warm and there's usually a bit of a breeze to keep them cool.

At 3am the dustbin lorry arrives and empties all the bins round the village. We listen to its progress as it performs its anti-clockwise tour of the waste bins before it drives off to the next village. Just as we get back to sleep the green grocer on the opposite corner opens her shop and wheels the trolleys out of the store room and along the road under our window. Because the road is bumpy, and the trolleys rattle, the noise instantly penetrates our dreams, forcing us back to reality. As soon as she's done that she sweeps the road and then washes it with buckets of water from the fountain.

We found the first few nights noisy but now we just sleep. It seems that as soon as you know what's going on you can ignore it.

7

A new century and a new life

All was going well. We enjoyed staying in our little house, dashing down at half-terms and during the holidays. Visitors came and went. We felt civilised. We worked on the house, built the kitchen units, tidied the bathroom and built a fireplace in the lounge to accommodate a wood burner. Most evenings we walked round the village after dinner, joining the locals, and we began to recognise people and were often stopped for a chat. Our French improved and we began to feel 'at home'.

We spent the summer of 1998 in our house and a couple of days before we were due to go back to England we were on one of our walks when we spotted a 'For Sale' sign on one of the houses that we had seen on the outskirts of the village. This one had stuck in our memory because it had a generous upstairs balcony terrace where, on our walks over the last two years, we had often seen the inhabitants enjoying their evening meal.

Fate was about to play another trick on us. We decided to ring the telephone number on the notice to find out the price of the property. It was owned by a couple in the north of France but, they told us, the key was with a friend in the village who would be only too willing to show us round. The next day we arranged a visit and were very impressed.

As we left for England our minds were in turmoil. If only we had seen the house in a few years time when I could retire, we said.

Back home in England we opened a correspondence with the owners of the house and began a bartering process. But fate hadn't finished with us. Owing to circumstances beyond our control, I was offered the chance of early retirement. We spent an agonising month putting various sets of figures together and finally we made the decision to take early retirement and to buy the house. We intended to keep the 'little' house in the centre of the village and to let it to holiday makers to augment our income. We started the laborious process of selling our house in England and finally, in 1999, we took possession of our new house in Provence.

Rebecca, our youngest, who had indirectly been the cause of our first journey to France, had a few terms to finish at school and so Christine rented a flat at home and we embarked on a 'to and fro' existence. We saw the millennium change in our new house and finally made the move in the following June.

La Timonerie
15 June 2000

Dear Mum & Dad,

The journey down to our new home was not too bad. Leaving England in the late afternoon meant that we were able to miss the worst of the heat and, since the auto-route was not yet packed with holiday traffic, we made rapid progress. Bendicks, was not happy at being shut in his basket and, as befits a bolshy Siamese cat, complained at the top of his voice for most of the journey, executing ever more heart wrenching variations of his complete repertoire. What is it with Siamese cats? Why is it that if we put his basket away under the stairs at home all he wants to do is climb into it and sleep but as soon as we need to take him anywhere he leaves
44

us in no doubt that he regards it as a prison? And like any good British prisoner of war, he thinks it's his bounden duty to try to escape using every possible means at his disposal.

When we stopped for a break we let him out in the car to use his litter tray and stretch his legs. It was as if he had been switched off, he was instantly silent and mistrustful of our intentions. He wasn't interested in food or drink, but seemed to think it fun to wedge himself under the car seats so that we couldn't reach him. And because we had one of the back seats folded down, he was able to explore the boot as well, although it didn't seem to interest him once he had worked out that he couldn't escape. In the end, in the interests of peace and quiet, we took it turns to sit in the back of the car and hold one of his paws through the bars of his basket. It seemed to keep him quiet and he went to sleep, but it gave us the most awful neck ache.

We arrived in the early hours of the morning and went straight to bed. We shut Bendicks with all his things in the upstairs lounge. Peace at last! Well, we think he was quiet because we were asleep in seconds and didn't hear anything until much, much later.

We had enough bits and pieces already in the house to survive until the arrival of our furniture, which was scheduled for the next morning. Predictably the removal men were late and it was just on lunchtime before we received a telephone call saying that they had reached the wine cave at the entrance to the village and were waiting for one of us to come and show them the way to the house.

We decided that the best thing would be for me to take them over the various routes in the car before they tried to drive the big lorry round. I did a quick guided tour of the three ways to our house, and each time the driver shook his head and muttered about finding a friendly farmer with a tractor. In the end he compromised and drove the lorry through the car park of the village hall complex, because that way there were fewer bends to negotiate. When he reached the corner of our road he changed his mind and reversed back to the hall car park to turn his lorry round.

Then he reversed along the road and round the corner to our house, finally coming to a stop outside the house with the lorry totally blocking the road - but at least the removal men didn't have too far to carry all our bits and pieces.

Just before half past two, I had to drive over to Avignon to collect our new car, a Renault Scenic. It was just coming on to rain and of course Christine had to stay behind with the removal men. I drove the new car back home, leaving our Citroën on the garage forecourt. When I reached home the removal men had gone, and we drove back to Avignon so that Christine could drive the Citroën home. Altogether too complicated, but it was the only way we could do it - and at least I had some practice driving the new Renault and was able to refresh my memory of left hand drive cars.

Now, we are desperately trying to unpack the boxes and find places to put things away. It seems that for every box we unpack there are a dozen more. We're not going to rush because we have most of the things we need for the time being. Rather than just make a terrible mess everywhere, we thought that we'd live in the house for a while, and get a feel for where we would like to put things. Honestly! It's not just an excuse for not unpacking or tidying up. We already have some ideas about the sort of storage we need and are going to start looking for some furniture when we go out next week. It's just as well that we did my study before we moved in because at least I can do some work in relative peace and keep out of Christine's way as she unpacks yet another box or two …

Bendicks is still very quiet and creeps cautiously about the house; uncharacteristically, he doesn't like the idea of exploring. He won't go outside and when we took him out on to the balcony he just turned round and walked back inside with a most disgusted and snooty look on his face. In England he seemed to enjoy lying in the sun, always finding the hottest spot, but here he seems to prefer sitting in the dark. All he needs, I suppose, is time to feel 'at home' and get used to the new house. I wonder if French cats 'speak' the same language. And there again, does he speak 'Siamese' with an English accent or does he speak 'English' with a Siamese accent and will he understand Siamese with a 'French' accent?

We have seen our nearest neighbours who have nodded a couple of times as they carry their rubbish up the road to the bins. Since the children here are still in school it has been very quiet in the village, although we expect it will be busier and noisier at the weekend.

When we got up this morning we decided that it was time to do something about the boxes outside the kitchen door. We spent the morning collapsing them and now, instead of a mound of boxes badly stacked up like a pile of children's building blocks, we have an untidy heap of cardboard flapping in the breeze - I don't know which is worse. We are going to go on a round trip of the village's rubbish bins tonight and deposit one or two in each of them to see if we can reclaim some space since it's becoming more and more difficult to get into the kitchen. We still can't use the front door because the hall is floor-to-ceiling stacked with yet more boxes and the garage is much the same.

I have taken time off to write this and we will post it this afternoon – our post goes just after four o'clock. I will try to write again after the weekend when we are a little bit more organised. I remember thinking, when we moved into our last house, that it wasn't something I'd like to do too often. I haven't changed my mind! How do people survive who move every two or three years - or do they enjoy living in a permanent state of insanity? I like to feel settled, to recognise the house noises and to be able to lie in bed and visualise the house round me. I guess it will take a week or two before we feel at home here.

How very un-English of me, I forgot to say that the weather has been fine apart from a sprinkle of rain on the afternoon we moved in. It's not too hot, but definitely warmer than in England and the sun seems very bright. We sit outside for lunch and have to wear hats to shade our eyes. The sky is amazingly blue and the green pines on the hill are magnificent against it. The bees are busy and the rosemary is in flower along the drive edge. In the evening its scent hangs in the air and mixes with the thyme that we walk on as we go up and down the drive. We have an old sage bush by the washing line post but, sadly, no parsley.

The chapters which follow are taken from letters that I wrote over the next two years.

8

Bastille Day

One of the biggest celebrations in France occurs on Bastille Day. Up and down the country, in towns, villages and even hamlets, Bastille Day is an excuse for a knees-up, a picnic, a ramble, races and games for the children and competitions for the adults. In our village it was celebrated with a whole week of frenzied activities, spanning two weekends. No matter which day of the week the 14th falls on it is always at most three days from one weekend. It is therefore only sensible to start the local celebration on the weekend before and finish on the weekend after. And if the 14th falls on a Saturday or a Sunday it is followed by a week of celebrations culminating on the following Saturday with a Grand Ball in the village square.

The celebrations for Bastille Day started early. The first hints we had of the delights to come were the large fluorescent posters adorning the shop windows and village notice boards detailing the village attractions that were scheduled over the seven days. These were quickly followed by the trailers for a fun fair that was to set up in the square. A buzz of excitement was in the air, not only amongst the young - for whom this promised to be a veritable feast of fun - but also amongst our redoubtable elderly ladies. The promise of a *spectacle Chippendales* in the guise of *Les Body Boy, Les Démons du Midi* was an unlooked for bonus, which caused much elbow digging and exchanges of knowing looks and whispered confidences.

The main celebration began with a bang on Friday evening – literally. The ceremonial firing of the old cannon, which usually had pride of place in the entrance of the Mairie, marked the summons of all and sundry to the *Place de la Mairie* for the beginning of the *retraite aux flambeaux*, a torch light procession around the village. Paper lanterns in the Chinese style, mostly striped in blue, white and red, and fixed to the end of a metre long stick were handed out to all the children and the candles inside were lit. The throng around the Mairie was swollen with visitors from both campsites and holiday makers staying in the village. The tiny children were not forgotten and were pushed about with lanterns fixed to their buggies, whilst the more elderly gathered at the nearby café - many complete with their own chairs. The procession was due to start at nine-fifteen, but true to Provence, it actually began to collect itself together at a quarter to ten. The event was led by a band, a mixture of brass instruments, clarinets and saxophones with a side drummer.

The band formed into a loose order and began with a stirring rendition of *La Marseillaise*. The crowd stilled, unusual for an excited French village, but didn't stop or stand to attention - although there was a murmur of accompanying voices as they hummed along. I was pleased to note that even I could join in with the words my neighbours were singing – 'De-de-de Dah Dah Dum ...' The closing chord was greeted with cheers and loud applause and then the fun began as a member of the Mairie staff detached himself from the throng and lit Roman Candles along the road edge. Blue, white and red flames illuminated the street and the smoke gathered and hung in the still air beneath the plane trees. The Roman Candles were placed on little holders and each burnt strongly for about five minutes, just enough time for us all to pass by. We joined the tail of the procession as it wound its way round the village. If the village were a clock then it would be convenient to think of the Mairie at six o'clock. The procession set off in an anti-clockwise direction passing the café, which was located at 'four o'clock' - its tables spread far out into the street and sheltered by the road barriers from the Mairie store, and came to rest with the band on the church steps at 'two o'clock'. Here we made a pause and a fire was lit in the middle of the road, around which certain of our citizens joined hands and danced. We were not quite sure if this was a patriotic gesture or a celebration of Provençal custom, but we concluded that it was probably just good fun since the band chose to play *Lily the Pink*.

The procession re-formed itself and set off again, past 'twelve' where the candles had been placed on the fountain opposite the *Grand Portail*, and all the way round to the main entrance to the *Place du 8 Mai* at 'nine o'clock' and which is substantially as it has been since 1789 when La Bastille was stormed. We poured through the narrow entrance and the band formed up under the spotlights at the near end of the square where a space had been reserved for the entertainment by *Les Body Boy*. The far end was wholly filled with the fun fair, two dodgem car rings, shooting galleries, hot dog stands and stalls selling ices and popcorn, candy floss and chips, whilst the middle was set with tables and chairs and a few benches for people to enjoy drinks from the buvette, a stall selling soft drinks and chilled beer.

The funfair was going full pelt, its loud speakers working overtime bouncing sound off the house walls and relaying invitations to spend, spend, spend. This didn't put the band off at all who continued to play, even though the disco for *Les Body Boy* was also belting out its music immediately behind them. After a couple more numbers the band played the *Marseillaise* one more time and then broke ranks. Not to be out done, the disco played an upbeat version of the *Marseillaise* and the band scrambled back. It took some experimentation to find a suitable, though not necessarily correct, key before the band joined in, the drummer finishing with such a flourish that he elicited a round of applause from the crowd for his prowess.

The band gave up and the disco swung into action. There were ten minutes before *Les Body Boy* were due to perform, but no-one expected the act to start on time. The lights over the 'stage' were pulsing through psychedelic colour changes, smoke machines were puffing clouds of smoke into the arena, the mirror ball was rotating and motorised spotlights cut paths through the crowd, swinging wildly over the massed village. A huge white trailer was parked alongside the disco and the lights continually flashed over it, searching for a glimpse of a *Body Boy* but the trailer remained obstinately closed.

The more elderly, who had brought their own chairs, made their way through the throng and set themselves up in pride of place ready for *Les Body Boy*, forming a barrier in front of which no one dared stand. Such is the wisdom of age. The little children invaded the stage which was a slab of smooth concrete on which we parked our cars by day, but which was used for al fresco dancing and other community events in the evenings as needed. The children danced to the pulsing stab of the music and a young couple joined in, jiving in the modern way - and very good they were too. Not to be outdone, a few of the more mature couples added themselves to the spinning throng and all the time the announcer spurred us on, exhorting us to wait for *Les Body Boy* who were just about to perform.

Half an hour elapsed and the dancing was still the only attraction. People were not restless, indeed they were very relaxed. Tiny babies in their mothers' arms, toddlers asleep in pushchairs, excited children on their fathers' shoulders, children itching to join the dancing, children eating frozen lollies in plastic tubes taller than they were, everyone was here. We said 'Hello' to the doctor and spoke with an American friend who - despite his rotundity - said that he was trying to round up a few volunteers just in case *Les Body Boy* didn't materialise, and asked me if I would be interested.

The smoke machines continued intermittent, irritated puffing as if they were just as anxious as we were for the show to begin and, as the music wound itself up a few more decibels, the tempo increased with Bill Haley. As the first shuddering chords of 'Rock around the clock' thudded out there was a parting of the crowd that would have impressed Moses and a couple joined the children on stage, giving a manic performance. Her shoes flew off into the crowd and his sandaled feet were doing wonders as the couple flung each other about. The young jiving couple from earlier came back, and gave an altogether more suave interpretation of the music, whilst the children continued to leap and prance.

Exhausted couples dropped out and the music resumed a calmer tempo, although without losing any decibels. A 'Latin' sequence took over and the Paso Doble produced some splendid posturing and much dipping of the ladies in their partners' arms. The 'Latin' sequence was followed by a medley of last year's hits and still the dancing continued. A large lady in front of us caused us to step back as, overcome at last, she was unable to contain herself and gave way to the beat, the massive gyrations of her nether regions threatening to cause us injury.

It is usual at these informal events for people to come and go as the mood takes them. They come as much for the social gathering as for the entertainment. The warm evening under the star studded sky was very pleasant even if the harsh glitter of the funfair and the musical assault made the whole process a little challenging. The music throbbed on and the lights continued their frantic search over the crowd as if they, too, were looking for *Les Body Boy*.

At last, nearly fifty minutes late, the stage was cleared as the moment arrived. The crowd closed in; there was no expectant hush, the music continued, track glued to track, but the lights stopped their frenzied search and coalesced into three pools of light. And then they were there. Three tall, athletic, helmeted policemen in black, body-tight Lycra shorts. Dark glasses firmly set on jutting noses, blue plastic jackets just open at the neck, they were doing the most amazingly suggestive things with their truncheons. The tone was set and everyone knew what to expect.

The children thought they were funny and aped the dancers' actions with their own imaginary truncheons, the older girls were ahead of the dancers and already had them mentally undressed, while the teenage boys were standing well back in case of audience participation, and the more mature of us … well, we were busy with our own thoughts!

It wasn't long before the helmets were removed, followed by the jackets, revealing skin-tight T-shirts. It must have been too hot for our poor dancers because these, too, came off in short order. Well oiled, muscular bodies continued to execute the steps to perfection, and then the Lycra shorts started to descend … The first number ended soon after, with several tantalising glimpses of taught buttocks before the shorts finally came off revealing bulging white thongs.

A series of solo and group items followed – there were seven dancers in the group – and willing girls were drawn from the audience to assist. Surf boards, sun shades and other accessories came on and the clothes came off. The crowd were not rowdy and enjoyed the entertainment, but we were left with the distinct impression that they were waiting for *Les Body Boy* to finish so that they could get back to their own dancing. The evening finally wound down just after 2am and a large part of the village slept in next morning, dreaming of …, well, it's probably best not to know.

The rest of the long weekend was occupied with numerous boules competitions, concours de belote, games for the children, and fascinatingly, 'jeux pour adultes,' evening meals and dances. The Buffet Provençal with local wild boar sounded interesting, and was provided by the village butcher - with dancing to the *Grand Orchestre de Bernard Touzeau*. Most days started with boules (Provençal rules) at half past nine in the morning, and their heavy metallic clinking rang out all round the village throughout the day in the square, in the yard behind the café, on the forecourt of the Cave – where ever there was a strip of gravel. The prizes were not huge, but 'mille francs' was not to be sniffed at - all the more so since it was to become 152.4490172 Euros next year. Vive la république!

9

Le Tour

I expect that like me, you will have seen Le Tour de France on television. When we were living in England it used to be on at the end of our dinner time and we often watched the stages that went through the parts of France that we had visited. Driving the caravan in France we have often come across cycle clubs out for the day and now, living by Mont Ventoux, we frequently see cyclists limbering up for the challenge of riding to its top. Incidentally, if the cyclists' support teams drive ahead, the owners of the shop at the top of the mountain will come out to greet cyclists who have made the ascent and present them with a certificate. In 2000 the 12th Stage of Le Tour came through Villes sur Auzon on its way to the challenging pursuit up the unpredictable slopes of Mont Ventoux.

The Tour de France came through our village last week and the event certainly gripped the whole community, immediately dividing us into two - those who had seen it all before and those of us for whom it was a new experience. Knowing something about civic pride, we expected a bit of tidying up, but we were not prepared for the effort that the village put in. It was as if royalty were coming or perhaps I should say, the President. The Mairie was given a 'wash and brush up', and new flags were mounted either side of the entrance door. Notices were put up throughout the village listing all the bye-laws that had been called into action to close roads, divert traffic and generally clear the village and its environs ready for the two events. Windows were cleaned and gardens were tidied.

Yes, you read it correctly - there are two parts to the event, only one of which is seen on English television. A day or two before *Le Tour* 'proper' came through the village there was *L'Etape du Tour* which enabled amateur riders to experience one of the stages of the great race. The 12th stage, from the Provençal town of Carpentras to the summit of Mont Ventoux, was selected for the year 2000.

In the week preceding *Le Tour,* a large number of pedestrian barriers appeared in the village, scattered along the pavements and in groups by the side roads. Earlier in the year, workmen had put in a crossing for the school children with a raised ramp like a 'sleeping policeman' with granite sets marking it out on the road surface. Before the great day came, the workmen were back making sure it was smooth and they painted white lines either side so that it stood out more clearly.

Flags began to go up and there was a buzz of anticipation in the shops and the cafés, and then little else seemed to happen and we began to think that it would be a bit of an anti-climax. On the day the amateur riders came through we began to hear distant cheering and applause. We walked to the corner of our road and squinted along to the main road where we could see a small knot of people gathered and the odd rider going through. We decided to walk up for a closer view.

Our minute or two of watching stretched into the best part of an hour. We had seen the outriders going past and shortly after we arrived the main body began to go through. It was not just a small, local affair - there were over 7,500 riders. Our stage of the race is a particular favourite, apparently, because it contains the challenge of Mont Ventoux, one of the supreme tests for serious riders. When the main body began to pass through they were riding three or four abreast, nose to tail in what seemed to be an endless stream but which, in fact, was broken up into sections of about 1000 cyclists in the interests of safety. They kept coming - we had never seen so many cyclists. Athletic young men, old men, pale white riders from the less sunny climes and burnt-brown riders from the south … it was one of the most remarkable things we have seen. The police had emerged and closed off the side roads with the railings and the traffic had been stopped to give the riders sole use of the roads.

Our village is laid out in a circle and the main road joins it on one side, twists round and then leaves at the other side with a sharp bend. The riders streamed through with some care but at a speed that we would not have thought possible, let alone safe. Groups of us were gathered here and there along the road and every batch of riders that came through was given a cheer and some applause, often while the villagers kept up their conversations. They seemed to be in 'automatic' mode, their actions triggered by each passing knot of riders and needing no conscious intervention. A few of the more hardy spectators had brought stools and chairs and were clearly prepared to stay for some time - and a few even had their picnic boxes. We could see the odd table set at the road side where the residents had come out, unwilling to forego a proper lunch.

We left after about an hour because we felt that there is only so much time that one can be interested in passing cyclists, all of whom are intent on passing by as quickly as possible. There was not a single spill or difficult moment in all the time we were there and the ambulances passing through between batches of riders had nothing to do - although doubtless, we thought, they would be busy when the riders began their ascent of Mont Ventoux. The sporadic cheering lasted well into the afternoon.

Much later we learnt that Mont Ventoux had indeed done its job well, and the ambulances had needed to summon reinforcements. When the riders were half way up the mountain, the weather changed suddenly and the summit temperatures plummeted to 2°C. Clouds, rain and fog descended reducing the visibility to a few metres in places. If you take wind chill into account the temperature was well below zero and the riders were not dressed for such conditions. Eventually the race was stopped at Chalet Reynard, about 5km from the top of Mont Ventoux. The summit was closed and the last 3,000 cyclists were unable to complete the stage. The medical teams treated over 700 cyclists for hypothermia and other conditions. At the time we were unaware of this because the village remained scorching hot.

The next day was a day of rest and the village held its breath for *Le Tour* proper. We had noted down the time when they were due and had thought to go up a bit early to find a good place to stand, somewhere in the shade with something to lean on we thought would be ideal.

As before, we displayed our ignorance and were surprised by the shouting and cheering quite early in the morning. The riders were not due until late lunchtime but the noise was well under way just after ten. Perhaps they are early, we thought, perhaps the schedule has been changed. We rushed up to see if we had missed it – and joined what appeared to be a carnival. The roads were all closed, police were everywhere, armed with guns and mobile radios, police vans were pulled into the side roads and security appeared to be high. And yet the police were just as relaxed as the rest of us, joking and talking, excited and watchful all at the same time.

There was a procession of vehicles going through with music blaring from loudspeakers mounted on their roofs. They were crammed with waving people who were showering freebies on the crowds. These were the trade vehicles, the race sponsors, the team sponsors – any and everybody who could claim some connection seemed to be in on the act. The experienced villagers had picked their spots carefully, away from anyone else by some obvious feature like a fountain, a junction, a bend, or even just in the middle of a straight stretch of road, and had set up their own 'camp' with a table for trophies, chairs for rest, an umbrella for shade, and a group of supporters, mostly wearing hats and T-shirts emblazoned with logos from one or other of the sponsors. We joined a group by the corner and began our own collection. In a short space of time we each had a cap, mine from an egg producer and Christine's from a printer, various bags advertising 'healthy' food, some with money off coupons, a leaflet or two, and quite a lot of sweets - although we left it to the children to scrabble around for them on the pavement - keeping only those that we caught, as much in self defence as from a desire to have them.

Mixed in with the cars passing through there were an increasing number of team support vehicles, vans full of spare parts and tyres, official team cars with elegant occupants, clearly out on a company ticket to make sure that the sponsor's money was well spent – on champagne, we thought, looking into some of the cars - and on immaculately attired chauffeurs. After about an hour and a half of this the pavements were littered, and the most successful watchers had enough trophies to decorate the railings and trees.

We began to hear sirens and shortly after, police bikes came through followed by the advance press and television corps, not just French services, but units from all over the world - although we didn't see the BBC. The police radios were crackling and a squad of helicopters throbbed overhead, thumping the air in our ears, which were already numb from the noise of the passing cavalcade. A few of the larger motor vehicles were stopping by the roadside to sell 'official' tour goods. And then it all began to calm down, the lull before the storm.

We knew the race was nearing because now the press cameramen on the motorbikes were sitting back-to-front on the pillions. To this day I don't know how they managed to support such long lenses and take good pictures, let alone stay on the bikes. Some of the photographers pulled off to the side of the road and took up positions in suitable vantage points or climbed the trees. There were a few more police cars and then we saw the first of the big TV trailers. All of a sudden there was a huge cheer from further up the road and the riders were upon us.

After the lingering TV shots that we had seen in the past, we fully expected to be able to identify at least one or two of the key riders, but in the event it was all just a blur. The riders came through incredibly fast. It seemed as if they didn't even steer round the bends, just leaned a little with not a touch on the brakes. The leaders were through in seconds and we just had time to take a breath before the main body flashed past in a huge pack. A blur of colour and heat and they too were gone. Another pause - just time to blink - and then the tail riders had passed as well and the helicopters were fading into the distance. Already the police were moving the roadblocks away and the first cars were nervously making their way into the village. The amateur day had taken an hour or so, today's competitors had taken just seventeen seconds to flash past.

Was the actual race an anti-climax? Not really because we did see it later that evening on the television, when we had the full coverage from Carpentras, through the countryside, our village, and to the top of Mont Ventoux. We are still left with an impression of the power and skill of these riders, their precision and courage. After the frenzy of the amateur day the actual race with its 198 riders seemed very tame and was over almost before we had time to raise our cameras. Perhaps the most lasting impression will be that of the publicity 'caravan' which we later learnt stretched over 20km with some 200 vehicles. In the course of the race it gave out 11 million free gifts! This 'caravan' included 1,200 journalists, 1,000 technicians, representatives from over 70 radio stations and 75 TV chains, 21 of whom provided live coverage of the whole race, totalling some 2,400 hours of transmission. There were 4,000 other followers in another 1,600 vehicles.

It is hard for us to appreciate the importance of the sport of cycling in France but we are beginning to learn. We will look with new eyes every time we see our elderly neighbour, who must be well into his seventies, taking his bike out for an early morning spin. With him we will hear the cheering of the crowds.

10

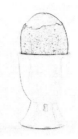

Hard boiled

Do you still have boiled eggs for tea? When I was a boy we often had them. Sometimes with bread and butter - well it would have been bread and margarine when I was little - and sometimes with toasted soldiers which we dipped into the runny yolks. I was reminded of them one day when I was looking down from the lounge window in our house in the centre of the village, watching the world go by.

Coming back to the boiled eggs for a moment, there were two ways to prepare a boiled egg for eating in our house and my parents were each experts in their chosen technique.

My father was a decapitator and with one swift slice of his knife the egg was ready to eat. Sadly, no matter how often I tried, when I adopted this technique the best I could hope for was bits of broken shell in the yolk and at worst, the egg broke and spilled all over the table cloth resulting in my receiving a good telling off.

My mother, on the other hand, was a peeler. I found her technique guaranteed more reliable results, though not without a cost and I can still remember how hot the eggs were when we removed our egg cosies – mine was a black leather cockerel's head with red wattles - and how the eggs burnt my fingers as I tried to peel them. One of the best moments was being able to bash the top of the egg with my apostle spoon. And I can still vividly recall how the eggs looked. We usually had brown, speckled eggs which, when peeled, disclosed a tempting mound of white egg ready for the spoon. I recollect, too, the eagerly awaited moment before plunging in the spoon to see whether the egg was runny or firm.

But the memory of boiled eggs was not yet in my mind as I was standing in our lounge window watching the world go by. Indeed, I was day dreaming happily - after all we were living in Provence and what else would a gentleman do?

A group of elderly men from the village were in lively debate beneath the window, gesticulating vigorously in the best Gallic fashion. My command of the French language was not good enough, and neither was my familiarity with the dialect adequate, to allow me to understand exactly what the conversation was about, but I gathered the general gist and concluded that this was a political discussion.

It became progressively more heated as time went by, and the mere waving of arms alone was no longer enough for the extra emphasis necessary to clinch the argument. Bread was lofted in the air as they conducted further variations on the theme. It seems no co-incidence that the French use the same word for an orchestral conductor's baton as they do for a loaf of bread. Perhaps, over the centuries, the baguette has assumed its shape for just this purpose. The argument raged on with increasing gusto and, it must be said, with the growing enjoyment of its participants.

I have seen such discussions time without number since they seem to form part of the staple diet of the elderly men and women of our village. These conversations are invariably vigorous but always good natured. Most mornings start with little groups gathering by the boulangerie, the tabac or the épicerie. Pleasantries will be exchanged, cheeks kissed, hands shaken and introductions brief. Enquiries will be made as to the health of all parties, each revelation being greeted with sage nods of the heads and then, the proprieties having been observed, the group will split up and walk on.

Every now and then, however, the discussion will be more earnest. The group will form into a loose huddle and everybody else will have to walk around them, usually in the road and invariably into the path of on-coming traffic. Either that or they will have to join in.

The ladies seem to prefer standing close together, heads inclined to catch the latest gossip which is whispered in low tones lest the Mistral should pick it up and carry it whence it should not be heard.

The men are altogether more open and collect in a loose cluster, backs to the wind, bread gripped in one hand, with the other reserved for the inevitable *Gitane*, those highly pungent cigarettes that they seem to glue to their lower lips, and without which, most men would not be seen out of the house for they are as much part of the essential couture as is the beret.

On this particular morning the discussion was winding towards its inevitable end and the group was eying the café opposite with growing interest – after a heated discussion, recuperation would certainly be needed, to cool down and take general refreshment if not fortification. At last the summing up began and the final statements to the jury were made. Closing points were added, some launched into the unsuspecting world from tip-toes, and eventually an accord was reached. It was almost certainly an agreement to differ since no-one ever seems either to win these arguments or to change their own point of view. Much nodding of heads, some shaking of hands and then the berets were off and the foreheads were wiped, after all debating under our sun is hot work.

It was at that moment that I was reminded of my childhood teatimes for below, set on the pavement platter, amidst baguette soldiers of bread, were six hard boiled heads. Protected by their berets, which had kept the sun from their heads, the scalps were shiny white but below, the faces and necks were speckled brown.

11

Music and moonlight

August in Provence is usually hot and dry. The temperature rises before we get up in the morning, reaching its peak just before lunch and only beginning to diminish after 8 o'clock. It seems a strange thing to say, but a little rain would be welcome, partly to save our having to do the nightly watering round and partly to freshen things up a bit. Most of the un-watered vegetation is nearly browned off and certainly very dry - even the established trees are beginning to show signs of tiredness and wilt by mid-day. There is always a leaf drop through summer here, but at the moment the trees are looking quite sorry for themselves. The rain will come in September and then we will have another two-month growing season. These last few days have been particularly hot. The heat ricochets off the walls and it is too hot during the day for sitting out. I took the thermometer out into the sun on the terrace last week but brought it back in when it reached the 50s and was still rising enthusiastically.

Over the last few weeks there has been an event most nights, at one of the cafés, at one or other of the campsites or just a friendly gathering in the local *sale polyvalent* – our village hall. They seem to relish lots of noise and clearly have not lost the capacity for enjoyment, and yet they are at work from 6.00am the next morning.

We've had a rush of weddings, too. Unlike the somewhat reserved British way, they parade through the village to the reception and sometimes even undertake a *lap of honour* round the whole village. It seems to be much more of a celebration here - the whole village joins in and even the passing cars honk their horns. I remember an elderly couple who did their lap of honour on a bright, lime green BMW motor bike and sidecar, suitably be-decked, of course, with bright apricot coloured flowers. They were accompanied by an outrider who drove most of the way on just his back wheel and with such high engine revs that his machine back-fired constantly.

And it's not only those living that have a lap of honour - funerals are also occasions when the whole village joins in. Advised of the time in advance by notices posted on the trees and notice boards, folk gather in groups under shady trees, in the café and at strategic street corners. As the coffin is brought by they fall in behind, accompanying it on its journey round the village to the church and then on to the local cemetery. These are not solemn times, although tears will be shed. Rather, they are times of remembering and of thankfulness for the life of the deceased. A table, draped in a black or purple cloth, will have been set up outside the house of the departed one and the villagers will each have recorded their personal messages in the book of remembrance.

The days are hot, the evenings are really balmy; we have been to three open-air jazz concerts in the village 'square' this August. The first was a gypsy-jazz combination with violin, two guitars and double bass. They played a cross between traditional Hungarian soulful folk and fast modern jazz. They were excellent, playing with verve and passion, one of the guitarists, in particular, was truly virtuosic and played with enormous clarity and speed. The empathy between the two guitarists was fascinating. They each seemed to know what the other was going to do next and shared the rhythm, harmony and melodic lines in an ever-changing relationship, as if it was a good-natured contest to see if they could catch each other out. We could sense the tension between them, the excitement as one made the challenge and the other picked up the cue.

The second concert was given by a jazz vocalist with piano, double bass and drums. She gave a very professional performance and sang all the songs in English - mostly standards by Irving Berlin, Mercer and Gershwin - a good mix of slow ballads, blues and well-known songs. One of the local village characters, Luc Travert, an aging man who has a dog that makes daily visits to the fountain opposite our house, was clearly overcome, as much by his evening's liquid refreshment as by the soulful and attractive young lady. For much of the evening he supported a conveniently placed lamp post and then he suddenly disappeared, we assumed for more refreshment.

But we were wrong since, when he re-appeared, he was carrying a blushing pink rose between his teeth, and very fetching he looked with his brown, swarthy face glowing with delight and his battered, black Provençal hat firmly over his silver-white hair. He took charge of the lamp post once more and proclaimed his undying affection for the lady as he joined in with her songs. Strangely, far from detracting from her performance, here in the relaxed ambiance of Provence, it seemed to add to the entertainment. Not for us the stuffy atmosphere of an English Concert Hall where even a sneeze brings instant frowns of disapproval. The young lady, who may well have known the gentleman, took it all in her stride and 'included' him in her performance to both his obvious enjoyment and ours.

The final concert was a Beatles soirée with the group *Get Back* and was as enthusiastically given as it was received – the closest we have come to a rave! We tried to decide on the group's nationality - they were definitely neither French nor English, probably a choice between German and Dutch and so we plumped for Belgian. They spoke excellent English, but with an accent, and some French. They dressed in the suits and wigs but unfortunately were neither quite as tall nor as slim as the originals!

They worked really hard, singing groups of five or six songs, 'back to back', very loud and accompanied by the obligatory psychedelic lighting - which was actually quite good. They broke the first set at eleven and returned in *Sgt Pepper's Lonely Hearts Club Band* uniforms for the second set. By now the audience was raring to be let loose and, aided by liberal libations from the buvette, they started dancing. Inhibitions were flung to the wind as the group broke into some good, bouncy rock numbers. The young were doing fine but it was the older generation who proved that they could still dance, and rock they did - with style and abandon. There were several encores before we went home at fifteen minutes after midnight.

Sitting in the square in the late evening cool, the concerts didn't start until 9.00pm which in 'Provence-time' means between 9.30 and 10.00pm, watching the moon rising amongst stars in a velvet sky and listening to good music for free - it seems a fine life. With a tiny effort of the imagination as I look around waiting for the start of the concert, I can imagine that *Madame, La Guillotine*, is centre stage and the eager faces sitting round are citizens – as, indeed, we are! The elderly ladies are busy knitting and we are straining our ears for the tumbrels. A little later, as the drummer is firing away with rim-shots in a really 'heavy' moment I think of the scene fifty-five years ago during the occupation, the troops in the square, the flag flying, probably draped down *Le Grand Portail*. The square in which we are sitting is named 'Place du 8 Mai' - the day of the liberation. If I think back further the buildings are new and the moat is still in place round the village, keeping out unwanted animals and invaders, our house would have been in pole position facing towards the old Roman settlement of Carpentras. And a little further down the road there's the lovely story of the villagers in Mormoiron, the next village, turning the bee hives over the walls on to the invaders - history seems very alive here.

12

Coming and going

People-watching is a curious occupation and there are few times better to indulge the habit than when waiting in a railway station or in the arrivals and departures area of an airport. Being in a foreign country adds to its piquancy. In recent years I have devoted many hours to this pastime. I am no longer unduly agitated about whether the train or plane is going to be on time or late, and it has enabled me to while away many hours that would otherwise have been boring.

Living in Provence has many pleasures, none more interesting than the constant comings and goings of visitors. I continually wonder where they are from, where they are going, what they've been doing and why they are here.

One thing that always amazes me whenever I am in the railway station in Avignon is the number of musical instruments being transported. No matter what time of year we have been to the town station in Avignon, particularly when the TGV used it, there has always been at least one person with a guitar casually slung over a shoulder. In the summer festival season there are musicians carrying all manner of instruments and we always extend our sympathy to cellists and double bass players who have the unenviable task not only of manhandling their instrument on or off the transport, or should I say 'person-handling' since many cellists are ladies, but also of carrying their other luggage as well. I wonder if they should be paid more money than the flautists and piccolo players who seem to have life so easy - danger money, perhaps.

Waiting in the thick of a crowd on the platform of Avignon railway station I was nearly knocked over by a man babbling away, apparently deep in conversation with himself. I was reminded of the man who used to walk through the village where I grew up. He used to roam the village talking to himself and my parents told me that he had suffered shell-shock in the war and had never recovered. Suddenly the man on the platform stopped and the people immediately following all bumped into him. Order soon restored itself and the passengers began to flow round him.

The passage of time has rendered this perhaps a more normal sight since the man's voices were not so much in his head as in his ear. Courtesy of Blue-tooth he was on the phone and talking to someone who, for all I know, could have been on the other side of the world. People no longer stopped to stare even though to the passing observer the man's words were no more coherent than those of the man in my childhood village.

Nowadays people seem to find the mobile phone an essential part of contemporary life and an essential aid to travelling. I wonder how people survived in days gone past without such a vital piece of equipment! In its right place the mobile telephone can be useful and even life-saving. But why is it that the 'ringing' of the telephone is usually translated into a command rather than a request? When did 'Is anybody there?' turn into 'Answer me now!'? I know that I seem to have an obsession with mobile phones but, in my defence, they have become invasive, continually thrusting themselves into my attention and, like a red rag to a bull, I find them hard to ignore.

Apart from those people about to depart by train or plane there is always the other group, and I am usually one of them, who are waiting for someone to arrive. We are a motley group, multi-national, of mixed age and possessed by startling habits. When boredom sets in, usually at Nîmes airport when the plane from England has been delayed a few hours by yet more trouble with baggage handlers, we resort to filling the time the best way we can. There is, of course, the café but it becomes impossible to consume coffee for the whole of a two hour delay and we are forced to find other entertainment.

Walking up and down fills a minute or two, and it's interesting to watch the different perambulation styles. There are the *arrogant* people who clearly wish it to be known that they are not impressed with the delay, who make a point of bumping into other people who are more patiently standing and waiting, and who find it imperative to reserve one of the few available seats by putting their bag or coat on it, even though they seldom actually sit down since they are much too agitated to be still. Then there are those who I think of as the *retired governesses* - ladies who half shuffle and half stride, eyes downcast, dodging out of the way of everybody else with a nimbleness that defies their doubtful age. Usually they wear a suit or a twin-set, often with a pearl necklace - Miss Marple would feel at home with them.

The *retired* folk are frequently expatriate British who have migrated here for the sun and the life-style. They make their comment on both by wearing shorts, the men usually opting for 'baggy khaki' while the ladies pour themselves into a pair two sizes too small. It is essential to wear dark grey socks with sandals if you are the male possessor of English feet - it would never do to be seen in public with bare toes like the French, particularly if they are stuffed into the first available pair of shoes that came to foot. The male torso is usually clad in a T-shirt, often grubby and proclaiming the virtues of beer, although anything that is not a shirt and tie is acceptable. The ladies usually continue the style of the shorts, seldom managing to fit the top that they have chosen, and in summer they find it essential to display acres of tanned shoulder, preferably just starting to peel like the flaking paintwork on an ancient, derelict building.

The hair is the crowning glory, however, and has to be a colour that nature could not have managed, even on a bad day, and in a style that defies gravity. Together they amble up and down, perch on the available furniture and endlessly look at their watches.

Not all expatriates are elderly and there is always the *young set* to contend with. Like the *arrogants* they occupy seats, not a single seat since they have to lie down, thus taking out three or four seats at a time. If they are not feigning sleep they have many occupations. The *studious* work through their folders, pen in hand, looking around to make sure they are noticed, and appreciated. The *executives* have their mobile telephones and lap-tops, the *amorous* their girl friends and the *hungry* their sandwiches – anything will do, it seems, to keep their mouths busy. And there are the *gazers*, lone figures who sit at the end of a row of seats, apart from everyone else, looking into space with a fixed, vacant stare. I wonder what they see.

Then there are the *beautiful* people - couples in their early twenties, their body language shouting loud and clear for all to hear. One young lady, fashionably wafer thin was artistically draped against her accompanying beau. He was a head taller and was artfully scruffy, a real masterpiece of understatement from the gaping shoes, via torn jeans, to his dirty woollen vest, the whole topped by an unkempt thatch of sun-bleached blond hair from which poked a hint of expensive sun shades, rather like fledglings looking out of an untidy nest. As understated as he was the young lady managed to be just the other, carefully underlining the exquisite way in which she was dressed. Strappy sandals were not enough, they were also bejewelled, and her linen trousers managed to stop short ensuring an adequate display of the rose tattoo above her ankle, securely chained in place with delicate silver links and an identity tag. Her silky top, as you would expect, couldn't quite manage the journey all the way to her waist and petered out below her ribs, setting off an expanse of flat brown flesh, this time adorned with a navel ring. The scooping neckline managed to thrust the huge straps of her bra into view although why her minimal requirements were so adequately provided for was not immediately evident.

T-shirts, and sweatshirts to a lesser extent since we don't see them so often in our climate, are a fascinating study. Mostly we don't notice the messages that they display. It may be that first thing in the morning they were carefully chosen or it may be that they just happened to be the next in the drawer but at some point each was selected for some good reason, the message important either for itself or for the aura it radiated. Beverages are common and so are football team shirts, so common that they can be discounted and American universities also fall into that category. Pop stars, surprisingly, are less common although Bob Marley does seem to have a universal acceptance and Elvis is still a regular visitor. Messages are popular at present although we can seldom read them since staring at someone's chest, particularly if the wearer is an attractive young girl, is not considered polite! Surely this must detract from the efficacy of wearing a 'text' but the really skilful restrict the number of words to a glance full, the wittier the better. I recently saw '96 rules KO' which had me thinking for a while.

And not only airports and railway stations provide opportunities for people-watching, sitting in the centre of a hypermarket mall provides yet another chance to indulge my hobby. The longer you watch the more you begin to recognise people, certain groups and families, as they make their way up and down the hall from one shop to another. The mobile telephone is active here, as well.

Recently I saw two men sitting at the opposite ends of a bench, one smoking and the other on his mobile phone. I wondered who was the most in thrall to his addiction. At first I thought it must be the man chain-smoking an endless supply of cigarettes, but I rapidly concluded that the other was equally addicted. Phone call succeeded phone call and when a lady, whom I assumed to be his wife, arrived even she had to wait whilst he finished the call in progress.

Last week a family with a teenage daughter caught my eye for no particular reason. The daughter was 'keeping up' but clearly not very interested. Shortly after they passed me for a second time, presumably having completed their errand, the daughter looking even more fed up with the whole process although the parents were in animated conversation. Back they came five minutes later, the parents no longer talking and the daughter looking decidedly mutinous. The fourth time they passed, the mother was clearly in front, daughter and father, now both thoroughly dejected, trailing behind. I would have been hard pressed to say which one, father or daughter, looked the more rebellious. And then, miracles having been worked, they made their fifth pass, the last time I guessed since the father looked relieved and the daughter radiant. And the mother? It was her turn to trail behind looking depressed. You can't please everyone all of the time.

I noticed caps and hats on one visit. The youngest boys, hand in hand with mama, were wearing their caps 'properly' with the peak pulled down to shade their eyes. The wearer having aged a little, the cap assumed a jauntier angle and, given a few more years, the wearer now sports his cap rotated so that the peak shades the neck. The years pass and the head ages, becoming more venerable, and the cap changes to a more suitable creation of plaited straw set firmly in place above a finely chiselled profile. No nonsense here, no mere protection against the sun this, but a fashion statement, a status symbol for those who would read it. The hair retreats a little further, lines of character begin to establish themselves and the hat begins to assume a jaunty angle, the brim now adorned with a wavy kink, anxiously proclaiming that there is yet life to live. Infirmity begins to threaten and the bearer has to manage sticks to aid the walking and yes, you've guessed, the hat transforms itself once more into the cap, worn 'properly' with the peak pulled down to shade the aging eyes.

In the frantic scramble for hypermarket acquisition not all is doom and gloom - trolleys are almost as interesting as people. I pity the harassed women who often have fractious babies and trolleys over-laden with what looks like a life-time's supply of pre-packed nappies. I envy the shoppers who have trolleys laden with fine wine and delicacies and I rejoice with the excited shoppers whose trolleys bear the promise of things to come. I remember an elderly couple whose trolley had a portable barbecue and a sack of charcoal and who were clearly anticipating the cool of the evening when they would make their burnt offerings to 'Al Fresco', the God of outdoors eating. After all, this is Provence.

13

All is not what it seems

The village settles down in September with the rentrée. The children go back to school and the adults return to work after their annual holiday. The tourists leave, the camp sites close and we can walk along the streets once more without being forced into the road. To all intents and purposes the village appears to have gone into hibernation. But it doesn't do to be deceived by tranquillity - the native Provençal is a wily animal and, like a hibernating bear, never more dangerous than when seemingly asleep.

We were working in our house in the centre of the village, tidying up after the summer season, when I heard it. I paused in mid-stroke, paint brush in hand, and listened - the whine of the siren was as unmistakeable as it was close. Climbing down the stepladder - painting ceilings was never my favourite occupation and seldom held my undivided interest for long - I crossed the room to the window and precariously leaned out as far as I dared to see what was going on. A quick glance led me to think that the village was quiet although about a hundred metres away a police van had pulled in to the side of the road and parked. The gendarme was nonchalantly leaning against the van contemplating the passing traffic, not that he had much to study.

A moment or two later I heard another siren. This time it was a police motorbike. The rider drew up on the other side of the road and acknowledged his colleague with a wave of his gauntleted hand. Were we in for high drama, I wondered? Was this the start of a thrilling police chase? Would they be erecting road blocks, throwing out those spiky mats to halt the escape of a pack of dangerous thieves? The tedium of painting a ceiling, coupled with the rarefied air I had been breathing standing on the top of the step ladder, had liberated my imagination and I continued to elaborate my fantasy as the officers slowly moved into action.

They waved down a passing van, signalling the driver to switch off the ignition. The engine coughed, shuddered, sighed and died, slowly and painfully judging by the twitching bonnet. Finally it grew still. The policemen spent some time looking over the driver's papers and finally waved him on his way, although his departure was not that prompt since it took him a while to coax his vehicle's reluctant engine back into life. Ignoring most of the cars that passed by, the officers singled out an old lorry, waving it down as before, and then an even older car on the other side of the road. As far as I could tell they seemed to be checking the drivers' papers and making a perfunctory inspection by strolling round the vehicle.

I went down stairs to my wife who had been cleaning the tiles in the hall and who was now watching through the window in the front door, making the semblance of an effort to clean the glass lest any passer by should think that she was 'sticky-beaking'. Because of the huge plane tree that is immediately outside our front door, the view was somewhat restricted, so we went outside and sat on the old iron seat beside the front door. It was one of those mild autumn afternoons, when the sun was pleasantly warm and the scent of the drying leaves falling from the plane tree was as heavy in the air as the leaves were thick at our feet. There were a few other people standing about, passing the time of day, and watching the police with growing, but casual, interest. It was difficult to work out precisely what the two policemen were doing but it seemed that they were concentrating on the older vehicles and randomly picking some to pull over and inspect.

In the distance we could hear the sound of a touring motorbike winding and roaring its way down into and through the village. It came on fast, swinging wide round the corner, taking it with style on the wrong side of the road - not the thing to do with the law out in force. The rider was flagged down and seemed to be having rather more than a cursory inspection. There were a great many gestures and he was rewarded with a slip of paper, which judging by the look on his face, was not the first prize in the police raffle. He went on his way with rather less style and a great deal less dash.

By now we were becoming aware that there was a growing crowd of people loosely gathering together outside the vegetable shop on the corner opposite us, more than was normal for a late October afternoon and, casually though they were grouped, they seemed to be taking a close interest in the two policemen and their activities. One of our local old men detached himself from the group and wandered down the road, leaning heavily and painfully on his stick. When he reached the policemen he engaged them in conversation.

He seemed to be on very good terms with them, and before long he was beginning to assist in waving down the vehicles, standing in the middle of the road and directing the traffic - choosing some to flag down and passing others on. The police were kept increasingly busy checking the growing number of vehicles he stopped. We could almost feel the bonhomie radiating from the officers - with the co-operation of the local villagers the tally was going to be excellent! Truly, this was democracy in action, and what a public-spirited character this old man was turning out to be.

The little gathering on the opposite corner slowly disintegrated as the villagers resumed their normal business. Some began to move down the road, chatting to the police as they ambled past although strangely, they didn't acknowledge the little old man. Perhaps they didn't want to interrupt his work or perhaps they were making the point to the police that they wanted no part in his activities and were disclaiming any connection to him. Some walked on down to the next junction, while others stayed up near the village centre. The people remaining outside the grocer's shop split into two groups - one of which migrated to our corner of the road - without stopping their chatter. Even the leaves seemed to be talking about it, picked up by the gentle breeze they were murmuring along the pavement.

A speeding lorry was pulled over and the driver brought down from the cab. He didn't seem to be very happy about this and was making his feelings obvious. Soon arms were being waved, shoulders were shrugged and voices became raised. The altercation went on for what seemed a long time. The other policeman crossed the road and joined in. The lorry was given a much more rigorous inspection and slips were written. After more gestures, and not a few words, the driver climbed back into his lorry. He must have said something provocative because in the twinkling of an eye one of the policemen was up in the cab and the driver was hauled out, none too carefully, and frog-marched over to the police van where he was pinned against the bonnet.

Finally, the police seemed to be finishing with the lorry driver. The conversation had become heated at times and we began seriously wondering whether an armed police force was such a good idea. After a telephone call on their mobile they wrote a sheaf of papers for the unfortunate driver who was then escorted back to his cab, shut in and directed on his way. He must have kept his mouth closed this time for there were no further incidents before he left.

Whilst all this was going on we turned our attention back to the other elderly villagers. By now they had spread themselves along the approaches to the village, gathered in little knots, talking and generally passing the time of day on this balmy afternoon. The group who stopped at the roundabout beyond the police check point seemed to be engrossed in a topic of such amazing importance that it brought them to a standstill. There was much waving of arms, obviously the conversation was heated.

Innocence hung in the air, much like the scent of the drying plane leaves, and as we watched we noticed that whenever one of their friends drove into sight in the village they were quietly re-directed down the side roads, emerging at the other side of the police checkpoint. In the same way yet other friends emerged at our end of the village having taken the back roads to reach us thereby avoiding the police.

Our admiration for the villagers was increasing by the minute; they were good, very good. Enough vehicles came through to keep the police happily busy and when an extra noisy tractor was being diverted, more folk moved down the road, chatting noisily to the police as they went, returning when the tractor emerged undetected at the far end of the village.

We sat there for the best part of three quarters of an hour, watching the village elders group and re-group - a fluid ballet of French farce. To this day we do not know how they communicated with each other but it is certain that the groups of villagers were working very closely together and we would bet on the fact that no one from our village received a ticket. Even with the stimulation of ceiling painting my imagination could never have given birth to such an afternoon of pure pantomime. We were sure that the police had no idea of what was going on … or . . . perhaps they did. After all, this is Provence …

14

Les voisins

As the years have passed many owners of old houses have sold off portions of their ground for new building. In this way the village has slowly spread out from its original fortified centre and the small farms around its perimeter have become incorporated into the village housing stock. The house in which we now live was built by a farmer next to his old and dilapidated farmhouse and when it was completed he simply moved into his new house, shutting up his former residence.

We have new neighbours. The old farm house next to our villa has been empty for a number of years and it is not a pretty sight. It's been for sale for as long as we can remember. When we first visited our house there appeared to be an elderly man living next door. Later we were told that he was just an 'itinerant' who had broken in and was squatting. The owner had some trouble regaining possession and while he was there the old man did quite a lot of damage, using the doors for firewood, burning them on a fire which he lit in the corner of the downstairs room where he was living rather than in the fireplace.

Various people have come, and gone, over the past year, walking round the house, looking at it, climbing into it and even being shown by various agents. Some of the couples talked to us - most saying that the asking price was far too high and the condition of the house was far too bad – all the usual things that people say before putting in a low offer.

It has been quite amusing watching the would-be purchasers since, at some stage the front door key seems to have been lost. There is only one door in and so to work round the problem one of the more enterprising agents brought a ladder and broke in through an upstairs window. He then opened the windows behind the shutters to the single downstairs room, and since that time everyone who has come has been forced to balance on a couple of upturned flower pots and climb in through the window. A few of the more obviously elegant ladies declined, whilst others hitched everything high and took the plunge, literally because the inside floor is quite low relative to the ground outside. Security has been maintained with a large brick placed against the shutters on the windowsill whilst the upstairs window remained open to the weather with its shutters flapping and banging in the wind. We're surprised that they haven't fallen off - their hinges are already half torn away.

A surprising number of the people who have come to look over the house have either been Belgian or Dutch although we also had a German couple. Very few of them have been French. Had they known about the lack of 'native' interest, prospective foreign buyers would have been well advised to be cautious since the French do not like paying over the odds for wrecks – although they are more than happy to ask for seriously inflated prices if they think they can get them.

Our segment of the village is very cosmopolitan. We are English, the next couple, further up the road, are French and then there is an Austrian with an Australian wife, an elderly Belgian couple, a French lady and another couple, one of whom is Belgian, but whose first wife was Scottish. Amongst the prospective purchasers of the old farmhouse there was a French lady who owned a farm on the other side of the village, but who wanted to move. She described what she was going to do with the property in great detail, and in perfect English - sadly, we never saw her again. Clearly her offer was too realistic and was turned down.

A group of three people came and looked at the house for a long time, a thin lady with a somewhat tubby husband and a young man who could have been their friend or son. They stuck in our memory when they came back a second time. They returned yet again last month and told us that they had bought the house. The young man was indeed their son, they were Belgian and they all spoke excellent English. They told us that it was their intention to fully restore the house and to use it for extended holidays. In due course, when the husband retired, they hoped to move in permanently.

Everything had been agreed, they said, and work would soon start. As far as we could tell the restoration was going to be supervised by a man from Paris who was 'very able and talented, and full of wonderful ideas.' They had already drawn up the plans and were going to bring the house up to modern Belgian standards for gracious living. Some of the work they were going to do themselves, but mostly it would be completed 'very quickly' by an 'excellent' builder from a neighbouring village. They anticipated that after a couple of months the house would be ready.

As if to prove their intent they began work on clearing the house that very afternoon. We had surreptitiously looked over the house when it had been empty and knew that they had a lot of work to do! We had also reached the conclusion that it would have been better to pull it down rather than to spend an enormous amount of money on its restoration. We estimated that it needed completely re-wiring, re-plumbing, new windows and doors, new floors and ceilings, re-roofing, insulation ... The list was endless and, at the end of the day it would still have no views - it was actually quite small, sat very low on the ground and was sited on a north / south axis rather than the more usual east / west. Consequently it was baked on summer afternoons and would be freezing in winter. They might have noticed that when its previous owner originally built our villa as a house for himself, he turned his new house ninety degrees to take full advantage of the weather.

They retreated in the early evening having told us that they had rented another house in a neighbouring village, and would be staying there for a day or two. They were back next morning and began to remove the tiles from one of the upstairs floors. This seemed to be a less than simple exercise since the tiles brought with them large chunks of the floor which the lady then tried to chip off outside the front door. All credit to them, they were certainly working hard. We eagerly awaited the arrival of the builders and their onslaught.

The builders arrived two months later in mid December with a variety of tools, which they unpacked into the house's garage having spent a long time trying to find the correct key to unlock the door - which proved to be unlocked anyway since all it required was a good shove. Then of course, they had to spend an even longer time trying to lock the door so that their tools would be safe. In the end they decided against leaving any of their equipment on site and so re-loaded everything back on to their lorry. They seemed very nervous about theft - they even took their drills with them when they went out for lunch.

The ground in front of their house is very soft, unlike our ground which seems to be fairly firm. We think that part of the softness is caused by the lie of the land and part by underground springs which come up a few metres away from the door. The upshot of this is that the ground is not firm enough to drive over. They discovered this the first time they drove on to it - and their antics in trying to extricate their lorry, which had sunk up to its axles, provided our first helping of their peculiar sense of fun. The performance was better than a silent movie and slapstick would have had little to offer that wasn't already there. They went through all the variations of pushing, adding their weight to various parts of the lorry, pulling it with their van, but all to no avail, the lorry remained firmly embedded in the now liquid mud, a quantity of which had been sprayed all over the men.

The *tour de force* was marked by the arrival of a huge digger which came just before dusk. Shiny, new and bright green it had a huge bucket on the front and a pair of fork lifting prongs on the back. It had huge wheels and tore two deep gashes in the drive as it came on site. It looked dangerously close to sinking itself. They decided against driving it too close to the lorry and instead hitched the lorry to it with a long steel hawser - the digger then drove into the adjacent cherry orchard easily pulling the lorry behind it and in the process it ploughed two furrows in the ground of the orchard as well as making another two grooves in the ground in front of the house where it had dragged the lorry out. Day one had reached its conclusion and so far no actual building work had been accomplished.

On the second day the men were prepared for the soft ground and came with a lorry load of ballast, which they drove on to the soft ground and tipped up. Unfortunately the lorry once more became firmly stuck. The digger came to the rescue, as it had the day before, and once more pulled it out, ploughing yet another two furrows in the orchard. While the lorry went off for more ballast the digger drove in and spread some of the ballast. We said it was a very big digger and its weight proved too much for the underground pipes which fed the lavabo and they ruptured. The lavabo, a stone sink in the garden formerly used for washing the household linen, began to grow a moat around it. The water found its own level by flooding down towards the house and flowing across the garage entrance and off along the side of the house. Several more loads of gravel came, the lorry was extracted each time in the same way, the water continued to flow and the orchard was slowly turned into an arena suitable for mud wrestling. So ended the second day.

On the third day an elderly man came and went quite quickly. We think he was the Chief of Works since he had a few rolls of paper under his arm.

As soon as he had departed the men began ripping out the insides of the house. Doors were thrown out of the windows and we could hear a great deal of loud banging. Clouds of dust began to pour out of the windows choking Christine who was working in our garden.

We were thinking of demolition rather than renovation at this point. Another van came and the sign on its side proclaimed its driver to be a wood preservation specialist. Our memory of the exposed wood in the house led us to believe that they might have been better advised to hire a curator of small insects. The man spent the day inside the house and as dusk came on the third day, everyone went home.

The wood specialist returned on Friday and backed his van towards the front door of the house to off-load his equipment. Naturally his van sank into the mud. The building team obligingly failed to return after lunch and the poor man was left with his van firmly anchored in the mud. He emerged at dusk and nothing he did could remove the van from its resting place. He telephoned and presumably was collected since he set off walking and we never saw him again. Not until Sunday evening, that is, when he arrived with his wife who was in a white shirt, micro skirt and stiletto heels. She was accompanied by their children and a friend. They tied the man's van to the car, an elderly Volvo, but failed to pull it out of the mud and so the whole group were put to pushing, no mean feat considering their attire. They all vanished at about half past seven and it was probably as well that it was dark since we doubted that they remained very clean. Equally, it was probably as well that we had closed our shutters since we feel that the wife may have had more than a few well chosen words for her husband.

And then it was Christmas and the builders took a break. Many people in this region add the Christmas holiday to the New Year holiday and take the opportunity to go skiing. We decided, in the interest of being good neighbourly, to make a tour of inspection to ensure that all was well. After all, the house was empty and unlocked - all sorts of damage may have occurred!

The builders were certainly in the 'struction' business. Up to the time of our visit they seemed to have favoured the 'de' phase although, judging by the little amount of work they seemed to have done, we were felt sure that they were also indulging in a touch of the 'con' as well.

There were now no floors downstairs at all, the ceiling over one end of the house, where once upon a time cattle would have been housed, had been removed and sadly the old feed manger had also been ripped out - the room was open to the roof. At the other end of the house they had knocked a huge doorway hole through the end wall of the house into the old barn that was perilously propped against the end wall of the house. 'Propped' because, although the barn was stone built and had a pan-tile roof, it seemed to be splitting away from the house and there were several structural cracks in its walls. It had clearly been added at a later date and had no floor, just trodden earth. The old wall between the back scullery and the only other downstairs room had been removed and the big, stone fireplace had also been taken out leaving in its place a huge soot covered hole knocked through into the barn whilst the chimney flue remained as a gaping black hole in the ceiling through which we could see right up to the sky.

We had to climb on to the bottom stair since there were no downstairs floors and the bottom step was a good half metre above the ground. On the first floor they had removed the walls between the two bedrooms above the former kitchen, and of course there was no floor in what would have been the other bedroom. The top floor, the attic space, had not been touched as far as we could see other than for some treatment of the beams by the timber specialist. We guessed that the builders must have completed the 'clearing' stage of the development and were going to come back eager to start on the refurbishment.

Denuded of any pretence of decoration it was easy to see that there was no electrical installation and no plumbing apart from a very smelly and dirty loo in a small room off the old scullery. There seemed to be no sign of a *fosse-septique* and so we guessed that they'd have to excavate the ground at the back of the house for that as well.

The builders finally returned. At first they seemed to be concentrating on remaining out of sight and out of the wind. They could hardly be warm since there were so many holes in the house. We wondered if the lack of comfort would motivate them to get a move on and start constructing something. There was a flurry of activity when ever the firm's foreman drove in and they were always busy early on Friday afternoons when he brought the weekly pay!

They gave us a friendly wave as they came and went. Perhaps they thought that they had taken us into their conspiracy, since they made little pretence to work when we were out and about.

The water pipe that they ruptured continued to flow and the ground immediately around the entrance to the house remained very wet. They put down yet more stones so that they could ferry their lunch boxes from the lorry to the door without sinking. They investigated the water main but, of course, the water main was already turned off and the ruptured pipe was a different line that came from the hills and had no stopcocks to turn it off. At some stage it would need to be repaired, but for the time being they simply excavated a bit more ground to try and drain the surface water away.

15

Thoroughly plastered

Gradually the workmen began to repair and rebuild the house. They started work – although perhaps that is too euphemistic a word to describe what they actually did – at seven o'clock each morning. By late spring they had built some new walls and rooms had been formed in the dingy void left by the removal of the old walls.

The crack of dawn and yet another disturbance! We had learned to recognise the rattle of the builder's truck, and had just become able to turn over and go back to sleep, but this was a new noise. One of the downsides of living in a warm climate is that the morning seems to begin very early. Looking blearily out of our bedroom window we discovered that the plasterers had arrived to start work on the house next door. Of all the tasks involved in building or restoring a house, plastering is the one skill that I admire the most - I find plaster is a wholly unreasonable and totally unforgiving medium and it confounds all my attempts not only to smooth it, but even to stick it to the wall in the first place.

I watched the unloading of the van from the comparative comfort of our bedroom and was able to identify most of the equipment that went into the house. A couple of crates of tools were followed by other paraphernalia; *auges* - rectangular black plastic troughs that all French builders seem to use, a couple of bath-sized tubs with paddles on iron handles that I assumed were for mixing, and a huge cauldron-like machine which must have been for mixing even larger quantities of plaster. The bags of plaster remained in the back of the van, secure and dry. All these items were self explanatory, but then they were followed by a huge sheet of thick plywood and a sheet of bright aluminium, both of which were placed against the house wall near the front door.

Having made a quick inspection of the house the previous evening, we were well aware that there was a great deal to be done. The men congregated in what was to become the new lounge and we could hear a loud discussion drifting up to us. This room was going to be a challenge since the electricians had merely 'stuck' the cable trunking to the wall with dabs of plaster, there was a sloping ceiling, and the walls varied between rough stone and crudely jointed pottery blocks, quickly skinned up to form a damp resisting cavity with the original outer stone walls. The floor was rough, unlevelled concrete and had various pipes criss-crossing it, some for water and others for the central heating.

The team set to with a well practised routine, fetching and carrying, planking the room ready for the first plaster coat, and making preparations for mixing. Everything seemed to be going smoothly, exactly what you would expect from a plastering team. And then the activity stopped. Angry voices were raised and much shouting ensued, followed by one of the men, the boss we assumed, coming out and talking volubly into his mobile telephone. Perhaps 'talking' is rather too polite a way of describing the conversation at our end since there were plentiful hand gestures, multiple shoulder shrugs and what we took to be a great deal of strong language. At times his voice was so loud that we doubted his need for a phone. Eventually he went back inside and then another of the men came out, slewed the van round in the mud which was to become a front garden, and drove off at speed. The rest came out and took a cigarette break.

About half an hour later the van returned, taking the corner on two wheels and ploughing a sticky slough to the front of the house. The man had gone for a large coil of hose, which he proceeded to uncoil from the front door towards the road and the new water main which had been installed the previous week, for, although the water company had installed the new meter and water outlet, the supply had not yet been connected to the house and so they had to bridge the hundred metres from the road to the house. That was not the end of their problems, however, because they didn't have the specialist tool to open the cover to the water metre chamber. When they had successfully improvised a solution to that problem, there was no connection for the hose pipe. It looked as if it was going to be one of those days.

Finally, with everything in place, they started the morning's work and we could hear the big plaster vat chugging away inside. The solution to the water connection had been solved but they had no tap and so, when they had enough water inside the house, they simply brought the hose back outside and left it, and the new water metre, running.

Throughout France, and not least in Provence, everything stops for lunch at mid-day. It was at this point that we noticed more activity next door than we had seen at any time so far that morning. At first we thought that, because of the late start, they were not going to take a lunch break, but were going to carry on working through. Now they were gathered round the 'eight by four' sheet of ply which they had balanced on the wall in the late spring sunshine outside. There was much discussion and some disagreement, accompanied by the inevitable pantomime, before a compromise was reached. They fetched another huge chest from their van, took out a circular saw and a couple of swift cuts were made reducing the sheet to a smaller rectangle. Leaving the remaining 'L' shaped piece leaning against the house wall they proceeded to set up the new, smaller rectangle on two trestles and brought out a checked table cloth. Boxes and blocks were gathered for chairs and a multi-coloured battery of cold boxes was lined up. A row of wine glasses was placed along the centre of the table accompanied by two bottles of wine. An old tin was set up on the crumbling wall holding up the flowerbed and an espresso coffee pot balanced on its top. The inevitable baguettes appeared and were broken. A bowl of salad appeared from one cold box, a platter of meats from another and an assortment of fruits from a third. Clearly this was not merely lunch, but the most important part of the day. We wondered how much work had been reserved for the afternoon.

They maintained a good humoured banter throughout the meal, which they seemed to be in no hurry to complete. In Provence the 'lunch hour' regularly stretches to two hours and then some - it is not unknown for the afternoon work session to begin somewhere near four or five in the afternoon.

As their lunch progressed our enjoyment of the spectacle was hampered by the sun's reflection from the, as yet untouched, sheet of bright aluminium. We had discussed this earlier and had been debating whether it would be used to bridge some of the more difficult gaps in the walls, or as a protection for the pipes under the floor screed. Since none of these ideas seemed to be really viable we had given up trying to guess its purpose.

Our thoughts about the possible uses for the plywood had proved incorrect, and our theories for the aluminium sheet were proved to be equally far off the mark. As soon as lunch was finished, and the coffee brewed, the metal sheet was fetched and rested against the wall adjacent to their newly constructed table. A considerable amount of manoeuvring and angling then ensued until the angle of incidence and the resultant angle of refraction enabled the sun's strengthening rays to tan the underside of the plasterers' chins as they relaxed leaning back against the wall of the house.

16

Mainly about water

When we purchased our house in Provence our attention was drawn to the water meter. It seemed to be in an unusually large manhole and when the two halves of its cover were lifted we were told that the water supply to the original house, now next to our house, had come in from the road there. We could clearly see the pipe entering our manhole and going across our garden to next door. Indeed, its presence was a feature in the design of our garden because we were aware of the pipe run and had to work round (or over) it. Our own meter occupied the other half of this cavern.

The construction of our new boundary wall meant that the water meter was now out of sight of the road and we were aware that we would need to provide access for the next door property should it be required. In between the building of our house and our purchase of it, French law evolved and it was no longer considered permissible for next door's water pipes to run across our garden. A new water connection would be required for the other house.

Our sleep last Wednesday morning was shattered by a ring on our doorbell and a few thumps on the front door for good measure. We were startled and immediately concerned lest such a rude awakening was the precursor to bad news. Our fears proved groundless because it was only three men who had come to install the new water supply for the house next door.

For once the weather forecasters seemed to have made the right choice in forecasting rain all day, and the sky was grey with a deceptively gentle rain falling. I say 'deceptively' because when it rains like this in Provence, although it appears to be like an English April shower, the reality is nothing like it. The density of the rain is amazing and within seconds you are wet to the skin. The workmen were well proofed in oil skins and expected, so they told us, to be finished in a couple of hours. Did we want to take our car out, they asked? When we replied that we had no plans to do so they left with a wave and started up their digger.

They started opening a trench from the new meter which the water company had installed on the edge of the access road a couple of weeks before and soon they were past our garden wall and heading for their target. The man operating the digger was quite efficient and it didn't take him long. We assumed that they were going to cut further down the access road and go in at the end of the house where the electricity also entered, since a convenient trench had already been left open. Not a bit of it, they had decided, or more likely, had been instructed, to go in at the front of the house, in the place where the old water main had gone in. This seemed less than sensible to us since the front of the house was somewhat cluttered with the remains of an old water well, complete with lifting mechanism, a tumbling down block parapet wall, two trees and a bubbling lavabo fed from spring water further up the hill.

None of this seemed to daunt them, however, and with the help of the digger one of the workmen easily uprooted one of the trees, and all its accompanying vines, depositing it in the middle of the access road. The parapet wall also offered little resistance. Watching the digger operator we rapidly came to the conclusion that he had passed his *basic skills* test and was fairly efficient with both the large jaw and the smaller arm.

However, he clearly had not passed the advanced tests of precision, gentleness, care and finesse that the team who opened up our wall footings had mastered. Exactitude was lacking. He didn't seem to understand the full significance of the word 'accurate'. Fortunately it didn't seem to matter in this instance since he was opening a trench half a metre wide for a 20mm pipe, no doubt just to be sure it fitted. Out came the disk grinder to cut a slot in the path and despite the continually falling rain this seemed to make an amazing amount of dust which hung in a sticky wet cloud over the toiling men, staining their bright yellow oilskins a dismal rusty grey.

Now it began to get really interesting because they had to move their van to make room for the digger. They drove the van down towards the lavabo, the digger following close on its heels, and made a start at opening the trench across the path and towards the house. We waited, knowing only too well what they would find.

The hills all round the village have natural drainage routes under the soil and every now and then these 'water flows' emerge from the ground, feeding little streams, little basins and other similar contrivances. In turn, these are all constructed with overflows which pass the surplus water on to the next location. It is a beautifully simple and elegant system which uses the natural resources to everybody's advantage, providing drainage as well as useable water. The lavabo next door was one of those points.

A lavabo in Provence is a stone (or if more modern, concrete) sink about a metre cubed with two compartments for water and a sloping table on one side where the good wives of former times did their washing, beating it and rubbing it on the ridged table and washing it in one of the compartments – the other providing the clean water for rinsing.

As I have already recounted, back in the previous November we had watched as the first work team arrived at the house and had wrestled with the soft ground and the sea of mud that ensued from the rupture of these underground pipes. And we had watched as the wood team became equally entombed in the mud.

It was unfortunate that the builders didn't remedy the cause of the wetness then, because it continued to create problems, even when they dug fresh drainage channels to try and remove the flowing water in the mistaken belief that if they later turned off the old water supply they would cure the problem. But the channels continued to flow with water because, as we knew, it had nothing to do with a functioning mains water supply.

Our new water team discovered something of this as soon as they had opened the trench to the house because it promptly filled with water. They tried bailing but they couldn't keep up with the flow. No doubt they put the problem down to the rain which was still copiously falling. They had a little rest and watched the trench re-fill and start to overflow, on to the path and into the house. By now they had worked out that something was amiss and so they moved the digger and tried to extricate their van only to discover that it had sunk in the soft ground by the lavabo. Rather than use the digger to haul it out they spent the next hour churning up the ground with the van wheels trying to push it out which, in fairness, they did finally manage but only after covering themselves from head to toe with mud and probably at the cost of halving the life of the van's clutch.

Like most of the builders the owners employed, this team came from the next village. That, we knew from experience, explained a great deal! Had they been from our village they would have known exactly where the problem lay and would have resolved it instantly. Come to that had the owners employed local builders there would have been no problem in the first place. And, of course, sadly there would have been no entertainment for us. But I digress.

The gallant team finally worked out that there was a connection between their problems and the lavabo and decided to open up the ground a bit to 'clear' the obstruction. Back came the digger causing, no doubt, a few more fractures in the feed pipe and they opened a hole to one side of the lavabo where the overflow channel is clearly visible and tried to rod through to make a route for the water. It was still raining and the roof water from the half of the roof nearest the men was splashing down on the path, adding to their discomfort. It's not that there wasn't any guttering, there was and it worked very well. Too well. And the water was pouring out of the down pipe. It was just that the down pipe stopped at the first floor level and discharged straight on to the path below, beside where the men were working.

The combined best efforts of the three of them failed to improve the situation, and they decided to break for lunch. In the time it took to bring their crisp new baguettes from the van to the front door – a mere twenty metres – the bread was drooping even more than their failing spirits.

Refreshed by lunch and with spirits restored they set to once again with one bailing for all he was worth, while another tried to build a dam with sand from the builders' sand pile and the third attempted to install the water pipe. We felt that he would have been more comfortable had he been equipped with sub-aqua gear. Finally, they simply back filled the trench and tidied up a little, abandoning the old lavabo to its own devices. As they drove off in their van we were left wondering if they had managed to stop the surplus water from entering the house, or if it was to be a feature of the new hall – an internal pool, perhaps, for decorative effect.

But these men were not so easily put off and a little later they returned with a pump which they set going, pumping the water out of the lavabo and on to the surrounding, already soaking, ground from where, no doubt, it instantly made its way back into the trenches. They worked for another hour up to their haunches in water, trying to repair the old lavabo pipe. They opened an even larger hole by the lavabo and then cut some new plastic pipe which they inserted into the old, broken pipe. After this they filled in the hole, more or less allowing for the skill of the digger operator, and pushed most of the rubble to one side of the front garden. They made no effort to fill in the trench over the path or to remove the tree from the access road although the driver spent about half an hour smoothing the rest of the garden with the bucket of the digger.

Unfortunately it was all so wet that the result resembled a badly iced cake. When they finally left about eight hours after their arrival it was still raining.

17

Le Bûcheron

As we walk through the village, I am playing with a tongue twister. How much wood would a wood burner burn? That was the question we had asked ourselves last autumn and in the event it had burnt a lot more than we calculated. But I'm ahead of myself; let me start the story at the beginning.

Our house has electric heating throughout and a large open fire in the upstairs lounge. The fireplace is imposing – indeed, it dominates the room, completely filling one end wall. It is made from pale, buff, Pont du Gard stone, with two side seats also made from stone, and rises from the floor to the ceiling. The hearth has two fire dogs and a splendid iron fire back with a pastoral scene cast into it. As last summer progressed we had ordered a lorry load of logs, and stacked them away against the rear wall of our garden, covering them with a thick sheet of polythene. We were ready for the winter and were quite looking forward to sitting in front of a blazing fire.

The winter began in earnest when the Mistral started bringing gusts of cold Russian air down the Rhône Valley, and began to shake snow all over the top of Mont Ventoux. Very pretty and seasonal it looked, like the icing on our Christmas cake although not as quick to disappear! The days were warm, but as soon as snow appeared on the top of Mont Ventoux the evenings began to feel chilly, and the night time temperature dropped below zero.

It was time to decide whether to switch on the upstairs electric heating or to use the open fire to keep the warmth circulating. We decided on the open fire – partly because it was easier to monitor how much fuel we were consuming, partly because it would make a focal point to the room and partly because we already had an adequate supply of logs ready cut, stacked and dried, or so we thought.

In the event our dreams of an open fire in the lounge were somewhat tempered by our need to breathe. Once we had the fire alight it burnt well with a window open although this somewhat diminished the effect of using it to heat the room. Closing the window raised the room's temperature but also filled it, and the rest of the house, with dense white smoke, which made it impossible to remain in the room and which necessitated the opening of all the windows, totally removing the accumulated heat. Realising that we had not yet found the ideal solution we temporarily resorted to the electric heaters and made enquiries about installing a closed wood-burning stove.

This was installed at the beginning of January and has given us everything that we wanted. The room is warm and we can leave the door into the upstairs hall open, so that the warmth circulates to the rest of the rooms. Even our bedroom is warm enough for us to need no other heating. But the stove is hungry. In order to heat what is admittedly quite a large room, it burns its way steadily through the logs and has nearly consumed our precious supplies.

On our travels we had passed two new wood yards and we placed an order at one of them, but after a few weeks we still had not received a delivery. We went back to the yard and they nodded and said 'Yes' but still nothing happened. We visited the other yard which was much more co-operative and we were able to bring a boot load of logs away with us but as soon as we gave them our delivery address they said it was too far, we were outside their area. Mild panic set in but we were still hopeful that the other yard would eventually deliver. Another week passed and still no logs arrived.

Each year the *Mairie* advertises tracts of land in the woods on the slopes of Mont Ventoux for clearance. Members of the village undertake to clear them, bringing the wood back for their winter use. The scent of burning oak drifts round the village in the evenings and is a winter delight, bringing with it hints of mulled wine and seasonal fare.

We were in the village early one Friday afternoon posting letters and Christine dropped in to ask the secretary at the *Mairie* if there was a wood supplier in the village. The lady wrote down a name and telephone number for us and we decided to go home and look up the address in the telephone book with a view to calling in rather than just telephoning since the accent would probably defeat us, particularly if the woodman was a native Provençal. On the way home we turned the corner past a row of houses, where one of the outhouses has recently been converted into a charming small residence with a living room and kitchen clearly visible at ground level and two mezzanine bedrooms raised above.

Like so many of the village houses there seemed to be an original grand house with several, smaller buildings attached, all opening on to the one central garden space. Going past in the summer we had noticed that they seemed to live a communal life and we were never sure whether it was one extended family or several, since they seemed to eat outside in varying combinations. We had noticed wood stacked in the garden and assumed that it was for their communal use and that the lorry, which was often parked there and stacked high, was used to clear a forest tract rented from the Mairie.

On this Friday afternoon the lorry was outside, piled high with fresh cut wood, and we decided to check the name on the mailbox fastened to the wall beside the gate. It came as no real surprise to find that *le bûcheron*, the woodcutter, lived there. It's nearly always the way in the village that people do not advertise what they do. In England you would expect a neat plaque advertising 'Logs for sale' but here there is no need because everybody knows everybody else and what they do.

We opened the gate, went in, walked up the short path and knocked on what appeared to be the front door of the main house. At first there was no reply, just the distant grumble of a sleepy dog. Since the door was open in the early afternoon sun, Christine called in and eventually an elderly lady came out. Apologising for having woken her from her afternoon siesta, we asked if we could speak with the woodcutter.

'You need to speak with my son,' she told us, and pointed to the converted outbuilding.

We crossed the garden and rang his bell, a splendid hanging one with a rope tail on the clapper. In due course he came out, wiping his mouth on a serviette and apologising because he was eating a late lunch. He said that he went up the mountain each morning to cut wood, returning when the lorry was full. He then had his lunch before making his deliveries during the afternoon. He agreed to cut and deliver a load for us the following week and said that he'd cut them to length for us when he arrived.

Monday next we had nearly given up on the delivery and were about to start making dinner when he arrived. He backed his lorry down the drive, topped up the fuel in his chainsaw and climbed on to the log stack. He cut his way into the pile, almost half way down, and pushed the cut logs on to the drive before continuing with the next half. A thin layer remained on the lorry bed and these he flipped up with his toe, balancing them against his leg and cutting them in halves before kicking them off to join the rest on our drive. He repeated the action with the second stack of logs, showering us with sawdust as he worked his way down. We noted his dexterity with the saw but were concerned that he cut towards his leg. We were even more concerned that the toecaps of his shoes had several jagged cut marks... Fortunately there was no accident and Christine's life-saving skills were not called into action.

Looking at the heap of logs on the drive all that remains now is for us to stack the logs in our new log shed. When we had the new perimeter wall built we had a gate put in at the side of our property which opens on to the road running past. The road is just over a metre higher than our garden and so we have a short flight of steps leading up to the gate and a 'landing' platform so that we have room to open the gate in comfort. The space below is to become our new log store. We have asked *le bûcheron* to make a second delivery early in the summer so that when next winter comes we will have a better stock of dry logs with which to do battle against the cold nights.

18

All in the April evening

When the weather was fine, we were in the habit of taking a walk around the village after dinner – it helped our digestion and kept us up to date with what was going on. We had a number of routes, each of which had something to commend it to our attention. On this particular evening we were taking one of the longer walks which led us along the main street, out towards the campsite and then brought us back in a loop towards our house.

It was a route we often took – not too demanding with plenty to see and, since we passed the Mairie, we could check on the village notice board which was on the wall just outside the entrance door. There was not usually much to read and we didn't always understand what the official notices meant, but it was possible to glean interesting snippets of news. For example, on this particular evening there were notes about the unusual amount of rain we'd had at the end of last year. Apparently it was so wet that the harvest of table grapes was rained off and the farmers were being invited to submit claims for compensation. The same had happened, we have been told, when a surprise frost ruined the first flush of the cherry harvest when again, compensation claims were requested.

We also liked to read the school notice board, which was immediately next-door to the Mairie. We were invariably fascinated by the mid-day meal menus that were put up each week. It certainly made English school dinners look a little tame. There were always three courses and across each week there was a varied and balanced diet on offer. The same meals were made available to the pensioners of the village at a subsidised price, the only constraint being that they had to buy their tickets at the Mairie and eat the meal in the new school canteen which adjoined the school which, as far as we could tell, was a shiny and pleasant cross between a canteen and a restaurant.

We walked on along the road and discovered that there was a new shop in the village, an estate agent. We had a good look in the window and noted that the house prices seem to have risen since we bought our house. As the properties in the village centre have been restored and renovated the whole village has started to look much smarter. There are not so many empty houses now as there were a year or two ago and when it is opened, the high speed TGV link from Lyons to Avignon will mean that we will become a more accessible and desirable area for smart country residences and weekend properties.

Along the road opposite the new estate agent's office there has been strenuous activity and the former village public toilet has been completely refurbished. It now boasts clean, flushing toilets, a fresh coat of paint and an emptying and refilling point for camper vans. The old fountain outside remains but has been smartened up a little although it still wears the string of lights with which it was decorated for the Millennium. The whole has been given a 'Mediterranean' touch with some rosemary planted alongside and a vine over the doorway. A little further along the road the big houses that once marked the fringe of the village and which had started to fall into disrepair are being restored, and one of them is up for sale.

Still further out of the village centre there is a fresh road cut in with four or five new houses, all occupied and decorated in the beloved ochre colours of the village. Not so long ago ochre was mined locally and processed just outside the village. The avenue of plane trees that threatens every vehicle driving in from Carpentras was planted to provide shade for the workers walking out to the ochre washing and drying basins. That trade has now gone, although there is still evidence of the drying pans in the woods outside the village.

There are a number of 'approved' ochre based colours from which we can choose to decorate our houses, and the colour of our shutters is also regulated. It might seem oppressive and interfering, but the choice is wide enough not to be restrictive and yet sufficiently prescriptive to give the village a feeling of unity. Surprisingly, it is not permitted to decorate the walls of a house in white.

We turned the corner to bear round to the campsite and passed one of the dilapidated, half-wrecked houses and stopped when we heard sounds coming out. We had passed this house many times and it has always been fast closed. The shutters were rotten and the hinges rusty, and since it had never been open and there had been no signs of habitation or activity, we had always assumed that it was unoccupied. Tonight as we passed, the shutter on the road edge was slightly open and we were privileged with a glimpse of the interior. The walls were bare stone with no plaster or decoration, although they seemed to have the odd plant growing out of the cracks in them. The light bulb dangled on its wire with no shade, not a particularly noteworthy feature since this was quite common in houses here where shades are not always fitted; and there was a table at which a solitary, elderly man was seated.

Feeling superior, we wondered how people could live in such conditions. As we walked on past our view of the room changed and we saw the man's wife taking their meal from a microwave, which was balanced on top of one of the largest fridge-freezers we have ever seen. On the bench next to it there was an equally impressive wide-screen television with a satellite dish balanced on its top. We looked from the cutting edge technology to the bare stonewalls, from the modern appliances to the rotting shutters and pondered. There was a quite different ordering of priorities here, and this was not the only example we had seen in the village. We walked on, wondering if we worried too much about the wrong things in life.

We followed the road past the campsite, which had just opened for the new season. There were a few vans drawn up by the shelter of the hedge at the far end, almost as if they were corralled against marauding Indians. The campsite was mostly deserted although we knew it would not be long before it began to fill and buzz with the early summer evening activity. The new toilet and washing up facilities were ablaze with light - and as yet totally unused.

Darkness had fallen and we headed out along the side of the football pitch, making our way carefully towards the far side where the road turns back into the village and towards our house. Seasonal movements of sheep were very common and several times each year we came across them resting overnight – usually gathered together in one of the fields at the edge of the village and watched over by their shepherd and his dogs, very pastoral and traditional.

That night we passed a horse tethered on the grass by the football pitch, hobbled to a peg screwed into the ground under the olive trees by the tennis courts. He snickered as we passed – it was a contented murmur on a warm night. A few paces further on we nearly fell over a cow, tethered in the same way. Now this was unusual since there were few cattle in our part of France and we had not seen a single cow in the fields near the village let alone one here, actually in the village. It was too dark for us to see much and we debated whether this was actually a cow or whether it was just a trick of the light and our over fertile imaginations aided, no doubt, by the glass of wine we had consumed with our evening meal. If it was a cow, we decided, perhaps it belonged to one of the villagers who kept it out of sight in a barn and who had brought it in before going on to market the next day although we were not clear as to why it should have been tethered there.

Another animal loomed up in the dark. This time there could be no doubt as to what it was, the shape was so very distinctive. Somewhat startled to find a llama calmly chewing its supper in the middle of the village we made a diversion round it only to come upon the tent of the visiting circus, in town for its spring visit. Lions, thankfully caged this time, and other exotic animals were in the space in front of the caravans. A huge power cable ran across the road, nearly tripping us up, and had been joined into the football pitch's flood lighting power supply.

We turned the corner, back towards the village and our own road, and heard the click of boules from the back yard of the café floating on the still air. Laughter punctuated the silence and then shouts of encouragement – clearly there was a needle match in progress. Just before we turned into our road we saw the glow of the lights at the village lavabo, way down on the main road. The lavabo, like the public toilets, had been festooned with pulsing lights for the Millennium change and we decided that the village must have made a bulk purchase of them since they seemed to have been draped over every available building.

Many villages have public washing facilities – long stone troughs with attached scrubbing benches usually fed with running water from a fountain, and they are still used. Going shopping earlier that day we had seen a couple of the village's redoubtable ladies washing a carpet in the stone basins of the lavabo and when we came back the carpet had been draped over the rails to dry in the afternoon sun. That evening we were too lazy to walk down and see if it was still there. Instead we turned towards home, a pleasant walk all in an April evening.

19

May 8th

You might be forgiven for thinking that our life was spent in constant wild and riotous living, but in May we attended an altogether different kind of celebration – a quiet time when the past was no less present in our thoughts but when it was contemplated in a totally different frame of mind.

Living in a French village is quite unlike living in an English village. For one thing, most French villages are tiny by comparison with their English counterparts and often they refer to a loose geographical region rather than a tight group of houses. The village where we live is compact and centred round the village square, but it also has outlying hamlets spreading out into the surrounding countryside like the fingers of a hand. And another difference is that villages are mostly populated by families who have lived there for generations. French property laws keep houses within the family and, where property is owned, on the death of its owner it usually remains within the family rather than being sold.

French villagers celebrate their culture. The French have a word 'le patrimoine,' which translates into our word 'heritage' but in France it means so much more. Not only does it convey the essence of being French, it also conveys a deep pride in, and respect for, the place where they live. When we moved to Provence we were struck by the number of people who told us that our village was the only place on earth worth living in. We felt that they genuinely pitied those poor people who were not fortunate enough to live there.

Apart from wine, I sometimes think that the other main ingredient running in the veins of the French is history. Wherever you find yourself you are steeped in history – it's all round you. Roman roads, towns with their fortified walls still intact, covered markets, ancient churches – every village proudly wears its past with its present. We were shopping the other day in a new, ultra modern shopping mall and we went into a clothes shop. Rising up in the midst of the glittering chrome and sparkling glass there was a massive stone pillar and a Roman arch leading to a corner of an old ruined building. How inconvenient it must have been for the architect and the builders, but its preservation meant that I can still visualise that shop.

The 8th of May is Armistice Day, and it is a National holiday in France. Amongst other commemorations, it marks the liberation of our village from its occupying German forces. As in many villages throughout France, the square in the centre of our village is named 'Place du 8 Mai' and is another potent reminder of our recent past.

Notices posted around the village during the previous week proclaimed that there would be a 'solemn gathering in La Place de La Mairie' at 11.30am, followed by a procession to 'the Place of the Dead'.

The morning of the 8th dawns fine and sunny and so we decided to walk into the village to post a letter and see what will happen. As is usual in Provence, 11.30am is not the definitive hour but an approximate time indicating when the event will begin to gather itself together. We notice that there are more people about than is normal for this time of year; many of them are elderly although there is also a generous sprinkling of young children accompanied by their parents. Benches have been set up outside the Mairie and there is a trestle table, bare but for a long, thin wooden box.

As people arrive they greet each other with customary warmth and informality, cheeks are kissed here, hands grasped there, an arm goes around a shoulder and a back is slapped. Little groups of our citizens gather under the plane trees outside the grocer's shop across the road from the Mairie and at the café further down the road. They mingle with cyclists passing through and people fetching bread from the boulangerie – some are nearly mown down by motorists squeezing through on their way to the next village, while others thread their way in and out of the cars which are parked in their usual haphazard way along the road's edge.

The crowd is small but begins to look business like. A knot of people have come together outside the Mairie, and are taking flags out of the long wooden box on the table and screwing together the sections of the standard poles. A long, memorial wreath has arrived, festooned with blue, white and red ribbons. It has pale yellow flowers, strangely unseasonable, threaded through a bed of greenery. It rests on the table in front of the flag box.

More young children are arriving and they are carrying bunches of flowers. There are fresh-cut iris from their gardens, tiny posies made up by the local florist and flowers that I cannot identify from the distance – misty pink and lilac. They are made all the more poignant because, as they droop in the children's lively hands, they proclaim the mortality of all things living – much more so than the everlasting plastic poppies and wax wreaths common in England.

The space is filling and people gravitate towards the Mairie leaving the welcome shade of the plane trees and the solace of the café. The procession isn't 'forming up' and there are no uniforms, no medals. There is no formality and people continue to chat. Some of the elderly are more smartly dressed than usual, wearing blazers. Others are in their normal everyday clothes – brightly coloured open neck shirts, jeans and the odd sweatshirt. The children are more neatly dressed and some of the girls are even wearing dresses – I suspect that their redoubtable teacher has been laying down some firm guidance, obviously to good effect! Shoes remain informal – no 'shiny black' to be seen, open sandals, casuals and trainers are the order of the day.

The crowd begins to stir. It is now twenty minutes beyond eleven-thirty. One of the council workers who does crossing duty for the school is gathering the children together – not into neat lines, two by two, but merely into the semblance of a column – and he leads them into the middle of the road.

They are followed by a small group of men including three standard bearers. A fourth is carrying the floral tribute, incongruously large since it is about a metre wide and will undoubtedly be placed at the foot of the memorial. The country's flag in the centre clashes with the bright, fluorescent green shirt that its bearer is wearing, and is flanked by two others. There is no wind and the flags hang limply in the morning sunlight concealing their identity, but as they pass I can see Villes sur Auzon woven on one of them.

The procession sets out with pride but no pomp. There is no band, no music, there are no speeches, and the citizens of the village simply fall in behind the flags, singly, in twos and threes, and in larger groups. They continue to chat amongst themselves, there is no silence, and there are a large number of canes helping the less sure footed on their way. Some people drift up and down the column, chatting first to one friend and then to another.

The pace is slow, unhurried, and they walk the long way round the village, blocking the traffic as they set off along the road that circles the village centre. Normally if the cars and lorries are held up for more than a moment there would be a cacophony of honking horns, drivers leaning out of car windows and general agitation. Today not a single horn sounds, the car windows are open but no one leans out and the village is peaceful.

Strangely, I find the atmosphere more reverent than most memorial services I have attended in England. It feels as if there is a quiet understanding here of what it is really all about, which has little to do with uniforms, medals, rank or the armed services but everything to do with neighbourliness and a genuine care and concern for the people who make up the community.

We are not treated to a cursory recitation of the names listed on the memorial by a priest with one eye on his watch so that he doesn't miss the magic hour of eleven o'clock – here the names are known because they were relatives, the brothers and sisters of the elderly and lost uncles, aunts and grandparents of the young. The simple handshake of two elderly villagers speaks more eloquently than many fine pulpit orations. They are not remembering names, they are honouring friends; their friends whose pictures are still on sideboards, lovingly dusted by those who remember them and studied by those too young to have known them, but who have learnt their history. Their absence is mourned by the people that they lived amongst and the presence of the young brings hope for the future.

There are newcomers in the village, as we are ourselves, and the thread which connects us to them is tangible and draws us into their loss. The villagers are used to people dying in the fullness of time because their roots run deep in the history of this place. They can deal with death from old age and even with accidental death, but this was something different.

My consciousness drifts as I look along the peaceful, shaded street and I see occupying soldiers, scared citizens peering through partially closed shutters and the odd child scurrying inside. A car backfires and for a moment I think it sounds like a rifle shot. Some of the elderly villagers wince – maybe they recall a time when summary justice was exacted. Perhaps it was one of their friends who had helped shelter a Resistance fighter or a fleeing soldier. For these people the reality of war, the daily presence of an occupying army, and the ever present knowledge that tomorrow they might be dead, is too recent and too vivid for them to forget.

Not just the last war but also the First World War. My imagination travels back to the French Revolution and further back still to invaders and occupiers that I cannot identify, my history is not adequate. I know that centuries ago our village was fortified. Indeed, our village house is built into what once formed the northern segment of its protecting wall.

Why do human beings never change? Today these children with their posies of flowers have learnt their lesson well. They know what it is all about. But tomorrow, will they go out and do the same thing? Probably, for that is the burden of human nature. We strive for that which we cannot have, scheme for that which we should not want, and treat each other with callous disregard for even the most basic human rights. It might not be happening in the tree shaded streets of our village, but at the very moment that our children are setting out on their procession, in other places, in other countries, people are perpetrating the same evils that we are condemning and corporations are caught up in the same power struggles that led to the wars of the twentieth century.

Much later, when we were beginning to explore the village, we visited the cemetery. French village cemeteries are not like the impersonal English ones and have family plots. They are usually gravelled and immaculate and the individual family graves are often decorated with ceramic pictures. The war memorial stands in the centre of the upper section of the cemetery, in the midst of the departed villagers and from where you can see the whole village ranged below. Even in death, and if only by virtue of their names on the memorial, these people are in the midst of their friends and relations as they keep watch over us all.

114

20

Thunder and lightning

Our house faces due south and sits on the top of a ridge with the mighty Mont Ventoux to the north-east. The ground to the south slopes away surrounded by hills so that we are, in effect, perched on the northern edge of a bowl. As I have already mentioned, when the Sirocco blows in from the south-west we are often covered by a thin layer of sand, but if the wind comes from the south-east it can bring prolonged rain and storms and once the storm settles in our 'bowl' it can take a long time before it finally 'breaks out' and escapes.

It is Tuesday evening and I am sitting on the terrace with a glass of wine in my hand, the sun is sinking behind the hills and a warm breeze is ruffling the long grass in the garden. It has been very hot all day and, despite the breeze, the evening is a little oppressive. The grass is brown and dried and I can hear the last whimpers of the Mistral, which almost blew itself out this afternoon, shaking the seed heads, a faint rattle mixed in with the rustle of the dry grasses. I am reminded of watching an episode of *The Little House on the Prairie* at lunchtime. The series is now quite old and the dubbing into French leaves much to be desired but the stories retain their power and evoke a feel of past times and distant places – something that we often feel here where tradition is still very much alive. With a tiny leap of the imagination I can hear the wind on the prairie, hear the rattle of the grass and see the wide-open spaces stretching away into the far distance on the horizon.

A sudden flash of light over the distant hills shatters my daydream and a little later a distant rumble of thunder echoes over the fields. Perhaps we will have one of those quick evening storms that can clear the air and refresh the greenery in minutes. The storm begins to build up. After a few more trial thunder crashes a spooky display begins with sheet lightning slashed through by steel-white and rosy-pink forked lightning. Then the rain comes, gently at first as if to lull us into a false sense of security, but then in torrents that have us running to close the shutters and fasten all the windows. Experience has already taught us that when the wind blows rain against the house it will come through the window jambs if we don't fasten the shutters to take the first sting out of the storm, and we aren't going to take any chances. We watch as the rain beats round and the lightning flashes. The longer it lasts the more pity I begin to feel for Noah floating in his ark. The storm keeps up, first on one side of us and then on the other as if it can't make up its mind which way to attack the mountain.

Some time ago, one of our neighbours told us that when a storm blows in from the south it often lasts for days. The last one split into two round us, each arm racing to see which could climb over the mountain first. This time the pace is altogether more leisurely and the storm seems to be in no hurry to move on. The rain continues, on and off, throughout the evening, the lightning crackles over the television and the thunder grumbles, rumbles and crashes about with ever more disgruntled outbursts. Eventually we go to bed and leave the storm to blow itself out.

Next morning the sky is overcast and the thunder and rain are still with us. We have breakfast with the lights on, the rain washing down and the thunder still crashing about like a petulant child kicking a ball against the walls of the house. When we open the shutters on the lounge doors we can see the rainwater running down the road. It is streaming through a garden further up the hill and the lawn of the new house, built just below it, is under water which is threatening to wash away the new hedge as it makes its way through and courses on down to the road. Fortunately, the camber on the road keeps most of the water out of our garden although we do have some running down our drive and away to the side of the house. Because there are no storm water systems, the roof water runs on to the grass and each house has a temporary swamp round its down pipes when it rains heavily.

The thunder and lightning continue throughout the morning and the rain gives way to hail with some huge ice crystals mixed in, just for fun and to prevent us from becoming bored. Then the clouds descend. Looking south over the balcony we can see three or four distinct layers of clouds, the bottom layer racing ahead of the others as if in a cartoon. Turning our heads to the west we can see through the clouds to clear blue sky and sunshine even though it is still raining on us. To the north the mountain has completely vanished, its place taken by a thick white screen, indistinguishable from the leaden sky, whilst to the east there are still menacing dark strata and flashes of lightning. The storm has abated a little but it doesn't clear until the last rumble finally gives in with a sulky clatter this evening. Throughout the storm the temperature has never dropped below the high twenties and the wind has been warm. After the storm, though, the air is fresh and it lifts all our spirits after the long hot dry spell. We go to bed, lying awake listening to the silence.

When we get up on Thursday morning the ground is dry again, the water has vanished and the grass, which two days ago had been burnt and dead, has new shoots at its roots like a green nine o'clock shadow. The temperature has abated about five degrees and now it is comfortable outside again. Tomorrow we will set to on the garden and resume the long haul that will convert our field into the garden we have designed on paper.

Neither of us can remember a thunderstorm which has lasted so long or which has had such continuous lightning. Our ears are still numb from the thunder and the cat hasn't yet gone outside. Perhaps he knows there's more on the way – I hope not.

We were driving back from Avignon not so long ago and were caught in a rainstorm. We have often commented upon the size of the ditches at the sides of the road and about the meticulous care with which they are kept clear. Usually they have a trickle of water after it has rained and we had always said that there must be more rain at some point to warrant such deep ditches. On this particular day we could see a huge dark cloud ahead which looked as if it was hovering just above the road. As we came into Carpentras the light began to change taking on a peculiar, electric green-blue tinge, and it became darker. Progress through the town was slow and as we came out at the far side there were a few spots of rain.

All of a sudden the heavens opened and the rain was upon us. Within seconds the road was awash and drivers were pulling off the carriageways into any available parking space. We soldiered on with the windscreen wipers at full tilt but they didn't seem to be making much difference. Strangely, because it was raining so heavily and there was so much water, we could see through the windscreen, which was washed clean by the flood cascading down. As we came into the little town of Mazan, the last town before our village, the roads were submerged; water washing off the fields high on our left was backing up and then forcing its way through any opening it could find to the lower fields on our right. The sheer volume of the water was too much for the drains and even the openings into the ditches were inadequate. In places the water was about fifty centimetres deep and so we had to pull to the side of the road with everyone else and wait.

The rain stopped as suddenly as it had started, as if someone had turned off the shower, and the sun came back out. In a few minutes the water level on the road subsided and, as the carriageways started to steam, we all resumed our journeys. The ditches were full, struggling to carry the water away, their size barely adequate. Back in our village the pavements were still awash in places and water was rushing along the gullies and gurgling down the drains. Where there were gratings at the junctions of some roads we could see a foaming torrent below and we wondered where all the water was going. The steam from the evaporating water hung eerily in the air, lurking under the trees.

21

Not just a school concert

When I was a music teacher, I was responsible for a great many school concerts. Even now my memory shudders at the recollection of such events back in England. The planning, negotiating for a date, bargaining for the use of the school hall, selling tickets, issuing invitations to the Governors, the problems of rehearsal schedules, setting out the chairs taking care not to break the Health & Safety regulations, car parking attendants, finding someone to do the refreshments; let alone the hassle of choosing the music, rehearsing and persuading the students to attend.

We have just attended a concert given by the local village school children, helped by a few friends. We came more by chance than design because there was little effort made to publicise the event. Of course we now live in a tiny village where everyone knows what is going on, more often than not before it even happens, so word-of-mouth is a very effective tool in the all-important matter of publicity. We did find a few enigmatic posters but, characteristically, they only announced the event giving no indication of a time or venue – although they did include the date. Our attention had been drawn to the concert by our American visitors, whose children had gleaned the information from their newly made friends in the village – word-of-mouth had triumphed yet again.

Our village owns a mobile staging unit, which the local municipal workers erect when and where it is required. They also bring out a few spotlights, benches and chairs. Local government in our village is represented by the Mairie and we have our own work force who cut grass, sweep roads, tend flowers and who, in fact, do any and every thing that is needed to keep the community flourishing. They keep their fingers on the pulse of village life and it is only necessary to talk to one of them about a problem and the information goes back to the Mairie and the appropriate action is taken.

It was no surprise, therefore, when we strolled into the village at 7 o'clock that evening, to find the staging set up in the square between two plane trees with one of the older houses as its backdrop and two tantalising views along narrow, twisting entrances to even older village houses leading the eye away towards the church tower behind the outer fringe of the village centre. The benches and chairs were in a heap just where they had been off loaded from the tractor-trailer and the whole deserted scene was bathed in the early evening sunlight.

At least we knew where the concert would take place and previous experience suggested that a starting time of about 9 o'clock would not be far adrift. We went back home and took our ease on the upstairs terrace finding some shade and cool breeze there – even though the temperature was still hovering just above thirty, it was a most welcome relief after an even hotter day. About five minutes before 9.00pm, friends from along the road went out and so we assumed that the concert was about to begin. We walked into the village and when we arrived in the square the first children, the 'tinies' from the youngest classes were already mustered on the platform and sound checks were in progress.

No matter what the event, no matter what size the venue, the village amenities are always called out and the sound desk was set up in pride of place in front of the stage, microphones were mounted on booms and the general noise level was high. The stage also contained a shiny red Olympic drum kit and a large African drum standing tall and slender at the back just like the pictures one sees of tall African warriors. By the time we arrived the benches had been set out in rows in front of the platform. Needless to say 'rows' don't have much significance here and frequently, in choosing where to sit, the shade under the trees is the first space to be occupied and not all people choose to sit near the stage – some residents choose the spot furthest away at the other side of the square lest the event should interrupt their conversations.

We joined the standing crowd around the seated area and looked for people we could recognise. Our neighbours' little boy was on stage and our American guests were seated a few rows from the back. The concert began with an inaudible announcement from one of the teachers. He left the platform, his face red with embarrassment, and the children launched into the first of the five or six songs that they had prepared. The level of conversation around us did not diminish, although we all clapped at the end of each song – some of us because we were paying attention, some by instinct and others just to keep their neighbours company. The children worked hard, facing into the late evening sun and synchronising their hand actions. They were joined by a few more children for the last song of their set, before being replaced by the next age group who performed in a similar manner except that, since they were bigger, the front row knelt down and performed the actions.

While this second group were performing, the first group, liberated from their ordeal, had a run round the square, re-grouped informally and performed their pieces again, more loudly, with more enthusiasm and much obvious enjoyment – long live polyphony and Charles Ives – at the same time as their elder classmates were struggling to complete their set. In due course the stage was replenished by the next age group, definitely older – the boys kept their hands in their pockets all through their performance. Dusk was beginning to gather and we could see camera flashlights going off as each new group mounted the stage. One camera, its operator leaning against a tree for support, had such a huge lens that we assumed its owner was an Ear, Nose and Throat specialist from the local hospital, but when we finally saw his face we realised that it was the resident who records local events and scenes and publishes prints of his photographs in the doctor's waiting room and other public locations. A young girl from the class on stage recited a poem, necessitating a lot of re-positioning of microphones and more testing, including a false start and a passing-fair imitation of the TGV, before she was able to orate her four lines.

When the oldest class took the platform the boys were decidedly 'hard' and very image conscious. The girls, true to stereotype, fussed about, finding their exact position and moving the boys into their correct places. We were not sure whether it was intentional or accidental, but this group sang in harmony, their eyes drawn to the previous class who were racing their bikes in and out of the fringes of the crowd, sending showers of gravel over the backs of our legs as they did their 'wheelies'. A lot of the younger children were becoming restless and parents were resorting to pushing buggies and prams to and fro in order to keep their youngest children from joining in too gustily. Unlike the more formal English concerts people were free to come and go as they pleased and no insult was taken when people left, even during an item. An older group of people were gathering on the fringes now, clutching their folders of music. These were the members of the village 'Chorale' who were to perform after the children.

Looking over the audience it was easy to see how busy the local hairdresser is kept with scarcely one head of hair remaining the colour that nature had given it. A quick count on this occasion confirmed that 'grenache' and 'carrot' were the current favourite colours with black coming in as runner up. The attire of the audience could only be described as 'informal'. We are used to seeing the doctor and the bank manager in open necked shirts, and even shorts, but it is at these events that the dress code becomes most fascinating. The 'retired' and visiting campers favour long shorts if they are male and smart slacks if female. They mostly wear T-shirts emblazoned with American advertising.

Young mothers are usually in shorts with the Dads looking much smarter in a clean white shirt and black jeans. The children do not wear school uniform but make an effort to be smart, the girls often in best dresses and the boys in shirts rather than T-shirts. Footwear is always varied, trainers, flip-flops and sandals heading the list with a few socks and laced up shoes. Provided it is comfortable, dress just doesn't seem to be an issue.

As the children finished, the sun was beginning to sink behind the houses across the square and the swallows came out for their nightly feed and exercise, diving and wheeling high in the sky and adding an extra risk factor to looking up. The lights came on and the string of lights over where the men play *Pétanque* lit up making a white stripe along one side of the square. The power line for the sound system and the spotlights had been connected to one of the street light boxes, as is the usual tradition. Normally at the start of such an event one of the local 'technicians' will arrive, break open the nearest box and, with at least a shower or two of sparks if not the blacking out of a whole segment of the village, will join in the cable that is then run out across the square towards the stage with no further protection -- we all just step over it and the children try to skid their bike wheels along it.

As the 'Chorale' took to the stage, the light came on in the church tower. With a splendid eye for such details, who-ever chose the light must have had a wicked sense of humour, since the tower glows with a deep shade of hellish red, clearly visible from the top of Mont Ventoux on a fine evening. Much to the relief of the choir member who had been standing next to us going through her folder continuously for the last twenty minutes, reading the order for the songs, checking that she had them all, closing her folder and then repeating the whole cycle, over and over, the 'Chorale' lined up on stage. They sang well but inaudibly, even though the microphones had again been re-set. Four men and about ten ladies who all seemed to enjoy what they were doing, watched their conductor attentively and shuffled their feet like school children (except that the children hadn't) when they received their applause. The conductor gave them their note from her guitar and they sang 'a capella'.

After they had worked through their set the stage was emptied again and a tiny boy – eight or nine, we estimated – went to the drums and moved them into position. At least, we think he did because he disappeared behind them and they began to move about shortly afterwards. He was joined by his Dad who played electric guitar *á la* Bert Weedon and they performed a couple of jazzy numbers. They earned and received a most enthusiastic round of applause.

We were then regaled by the Pensioners Choir. It took us a while to understand what was going on because they seemed to be gathering not to perform, but rather because the stage was a nice empty place to stand and have a chat. Eventually another elderly citizen joined them with a violin. This he unpacked with great care, polishing it lovingly with his cloth and finding a safe place to rest it. The group then played a version of musical chairs, with no music and no chairs, before settling on suitable standing positions. The leader picked up his violin and played a few notes, looking as puzzled as the rest of the choir. At no point did he go through the motions of anything that could be interpreted, even generously, as tuning. We assumed that this process was to arrive at a note from which they could sing because suddenly they burst forth, quite well despite the inauspicious start, and their leader immediately put down his violin and performed. I say 'performed' because he certainly didn't conduct or direct. His actions could best be described either as wringing his hands and squirming with distress, or equally plausibly, writhing with delight. No mean achievement for an octogenarian.

The song was greeted with tumultuous applause – we hadn't noticed the audience slipping away to the café for sustenance, but it sounded as if they had and, moreover, had returned suitable fortified! The whole process was repeated for the next song – musical chairs, more notes from the violin, discussions as to which song they were going to sing, and then a surprise attack as before. Again, the performance was rewarded with deafening applause. The next shuffle resulted in a lady emerging as 'winner' and she took up her position by one of the microphones. Cue technician, who gave a repeat performance of the 'adjusting the microphone' act. This time the note gathering exercise seemed to be less successful because the poor lady who sang didn't find a recognisable note from which to start, and we never discovered which scale system she was using. It mattered little, however, because she was rewarded with equally loud applause. Whilst she was struggling to establish her musical credentials, we had noticed a seedy looking character sliding through the crowd, keeping a low profile and making towards the stage clutching a suspicious black instrument case to his chest.

We were hoping that he was going to end our misery, little suspecting that he was going to add to it. As the applause died down he opened his case and we winced, waiting for the spray of bullets, but instead he sprang on to the stage with his guitar at the ready. A flourish of opening chords, however, did nothing to put the good lady off who continued chatting to her neighbour on the stage. He repeated the exercise and suddenly she seemed to come to life – her stance had previously been as lifeless as her singing – and immediately joined in, unfortunately not in his key, but rather in the one that she was promoting for the evening. A discussion ensued and we think that the guitarist must have prevailed because the third attempt was definitely a minor improvement.

We found the lady from the flower shop during this item and had a chat about the quilts that Christine is making for her shop, played with her new baby and then eased ourselves out of the throng as she made towards her home. We looked back on the square – alive with activity, of which just one tiny part was the concert, bathed in the last dying rays of the gold and rose sunlight which was picking out the details of the decaying stucco, the stars already out and the moon riding high, the cicadas joining in, the church tower glowing behind the roofs. All just a little different from the school concerts I remember.

As we walked home the singing stopped and the pensioners were replaced by a rock group who had the audible support of the younger members of the audience. Perhaps they were the owners of the large African drum which, when we left, was still standing, awaiting its prey in splendid isolation, or perhaps this was to be called into use later – concerts here usually run until mid-night. Looking towards Mont Ventoux we noticed that there must have been a car rally or some such event because we could see a stream of car headlights along the zigzag road leading to the top and the mid-summer fire beacons were alight in the villages at its feet. Later, sitting once more on our upstairs terrace, refreshed by something cool in a glass, we could hear the last notes of the concert drifting over the nearly quiet village. Patrick Tricot, a local recorder maker and player of distinction, was performing with his MIDI-recorder; live liquid golden notes cascading through the lines of counterpoint that he had recorded earlier, a Provençal folk song in a twenty-first century arrangement, a twenty-first century recorder in an ancient setting.

22

At the beach

Living but an hour's drive from the Mediterranean, towards the edge of a flat inland plain at the foot of Mont Ventoux, we are often aware of the changing wind directions. I am told that, geographically speaking, our village lies on the northern fringe of the Sahara desert. That may or may not be true but it's certain that when the Sirocco roars in from the south it often covers us with a thin layer of orange sand. Driven by the wind it goes everywhere, it invades the car and insinuates itself beneath the doors and round the windows; and if there's rain with the wind it takes days to remove its orange stain from the garden furniture.

We have always enjoyed French beaches, and when the children were small we used to spend one or two weeks every year lying in the sun along the Atlantic coast where the surf rolls in and the lagoons in the sand were warm and safe for the children. We have also been to the Mediterranean, but we have mixed memories of our visit. Certainly the sea was an unbelievable blue, but the wind was too playful and it whipped the dry sand into an uncomfortably abrasive blast which left our faces stinging. Since moving here we have been able to visit the Mediterranean in the off-peak season. With the help of a windbreak strategically placed it is even possible to enjoy the beach on a less than calm day.

When there is no wind nothing beats lying on the sand at the sea's edge, warmed by the sun and lulled into a near comatose condition by the steady ripple of the waves along the sea line. Besides unravelling the threads of our troubled minds the beach is a fantastic place to observe humanity in all its splendid eccentricity. As soon as people take the definitive step from the slipway to the sand they seem to transform into entirely different human beings. They leave behind their sober nature and become silly, excitable, child-like, lazy, and stupid – almost every quality that you can think of will be on show. The beach is a microcosm of the human condition and it never fails to entertain me. I have heard people say that lying on a beach is the most boring thing that they can think of, and I can only suppose that they mean lying on the beach with their eyes closed because I seldom find the beach uninteresting.

The last time we were there, for example, I noticed a little boy walking by, bent double by the effort of supporting the weight of a huge knapsack on his back. The promise of a good day's fun was enough to harness him willingly to a load that would normally have been considered too much for a single beast of burden. And then, a moment or two later, a man walked by. He was straight backed and walking along with ease. He, too, had a huge knapsack on his back, larger if possible than the little boy's had been. How did he stride along so easily? What was his secret? The load was more than counter-balanced by his huge belly.

On a slightly chilly day, early in the season, we were at the beach enjoying its peace and quiet. The sun was out and if it had not been for the wind, it would have been warm. But as it was, the wind was steadily blowing along the beach and we were glad of the protection our windbreak afforded, which gave not only shelter from the wind, but also helped to trap the warmth of the sun, making the leeward side tolerably comfortable. A very pale family were just down the beach from us, the mother sitting on a little beach chair with her children's damp towels firmly wrapped round her legs. With her sunglasses perched precariously on her nose she was defying the wind as it tried to rip the pages from her book. Her husband was bravely - or foolishly according to your point of view - digging buckets of sand away from the moat that he was constructing for the castle he had built for his two sons.

Sadly, they seemed to be less fired with energy than their father. Their thin and slightly blue bodies were shivering in the wind. The elder had been to the sea and was still wet, although the wind was effecting a quick dry.

'We're here to have fun' their father said through chattering teeth.

'You will enjoy yourself' I almost heard him add.

'But we're cold,' the elder son protested. 'Can't we put our clothes back on?'

'When we're at the beach we always wear our bathers. It's fun!'

We thought that this oh-so-British father had really missed the point.

On another occasion my eye was drawn to a lady standing on her beach towel. She was busily applying a liberal coating of sun block to herself and her ensuing contortions were sufficiently entertaining to make me glad that she had not asked her partner to assist. Part of her problem seemed to be that she wanted to be covered from head to foot but was finding it difficult to spread the lotion beneath her bikini top, modesty forbidding her to take liberties. Finally, however, after prolonged effort, she seemed to be happy that her protection was complete and invincible. She lay back on her towel and immediately sat up again. What had she forgotten, I wondered? Was there a square centimetre that had escaped? Apparently not because she took off her bikini top and stretched back out in the sun.

The problem of changing clothes on the beach has provided material for comedians for as long as I can remember and was the staple fare of those saucy postcards that used to be so popular, but comic inventions pale into insignificance compared with the real thing. Everybody approaches this thorny matter in their own way. We, for example, come prepared already wearing our beach clothes and when we get them wet we lie in the sun until they are dry. It seems a very simple solution to what for many people is a major problem. We like to arrive early in the morning when the beach is nearly always empty and we tuck ourselves out of the way, usually up against the top of the beach where the sand is dry and the people trekking by do not trample us as we lie in the sun.

But as the day progresses the beach fills up. The choice places are long gone and the second and third rows are in place, more if the tide is out, and space becomes difficult to find. About this time the beach population begins to change. The early morning brigade, who have come for a swim, pack up and go and the office workers come for their extended lunch hour break. They are efficient and practised in the ritual. One simple shoulder bag, a towel, a baguette, a bottle of water and a book is all they need. The towel is spread, exactly flat, defining their space, the clothes are removed and the body is laid on the towel. Sun glasses are essential and the baguette is torn apart and consumed, rather like medicine, with gulps of water from the bottle. The repast finished they turn on to their stomachs and read for half an hour.

As if by some magic internal alarm, they close the book and make their way to the sea for partial immersion – only partial because it is essential to keep the hair neat and dry. Back on their towel they lie on their backs and toast for another half hour. Once more the internal alarm goes off, they dress and depart, as neat and tidy as when they arrived. Their departure signals the arrival of the families, the time when anything can, and usually does, happen.

I remember a crowd of young boys who settled not far from us. They were noisy and their raucous shouts drifted up to us as they were splashing about in the sea. Back on the beach, they settled down, plugged their ears into their Walkmans and drifted into silence. Silence perhaps, but their eyes were alert and they were studying everyone around them. As if by a magnet, their attention was drawn to a somewhat buxom woman who was in the process of changing. Not for her the modest wriggle behind a towel – she bared all, struck a pose as if to say 'Look at me!' and then pulled on a very tiny costume. The boys looked away in disgust.

A little while later another young woman arrived and the process of changing began again. The more she covered herself, and the more the towel covered, the more their attention became riveted. The old adage seems to be true – the more you have the less you want and the less you have the more you crave.

23

The fountain

In our hot, dry climate the splash of running water is one of the most inviting and welcoming sounds imaginable, and our village is blest by having a large number of fountains fed with cool water rising from natural springs which are, in turn, replenished by water from the mountain. Having free running water is a valuable asset and one which man and beast are not slow to use to their advantage whether it be for a quick drink, for the weekly washing or just for watering the pot plants.

Much of the village life hinges around one or other of the fountains where people still meet in time honoured tradition for a chat whilst they fill their containers. Our village centre house was opposite a splendid stone fountain which has two spouts, rails to support a bucket or container, and a deep water basin rising nearly a metre from the ground. The carved centre of the fountain stands about two and a half metres tall and faces down the main road away from the centre of the village It is a striking, though not particularly elaborate or handsome, feature which continually gushes steady streams of crystal clear water.

During the summer letting season we would spend the change-over morning for the guests at our village house cleaning and changing beds so that by the afternoon we were ready and waiting for the next batch of visitors. There was an iron bench outside the house, in the shade of a

plane tree, which looked down the road along which the new-comers
would arrive, and we would sit there waiting to greet them.

Just before lunch our attention was caught by a car which veered across the road and hastily parked across the junction. A short, elderly man leaped out of the car, leaving the engine running, and dashed the remaining few metres to the fountain, where he dexterously extracted his false teeth and dunked them in the basin of the fountain. His wife followed at a more measured pace bringing toothpaste and a brush.

After a quick clean and a sluicing in the basin – not for him the crystal clear stream of water pouring from the spout – the teeth were restored to their customary place and, with a trial grin and a practice gnash to ascertain their correct alignment, the man returned to the car, followed as before, by his wife with the toothpaste and brush. They slammed the car doors, the gears were noisily engaged and they drove off. To this day we do not know whether it was something he ate or whether it was something he said although, judging by the look on his wife's face, we inclined to the latter.

This in itself would have been sufficiently diverting to amuse us, but coming as it did after a busy morning the moment was enhanced by what had gone before. They say that ignorance is bliss – never was a truer word spoken for earlier in the day there had been the usual succession of visitors to the fountain. This was not unusual for a Saturday morning but clearly the couple in the car had not been aware of them.

On a summer Saturday a steady succession of cyclists is drawn to our village partly because we are sited at one end of the *Gorges de la Nesque,* and partly by our proximity to *Mont Ventoux.* They are attracted by the straight roads into the village, the winding road through the *Gorges de la Nesque* – which in places is cut through the rock and clings precariously to the steep sides of the gorge – and, of course, by the challenge of the road leading to the top of the mountain. With its spectacular bends, which climb to just over 1900 metres, and the lunar views at the summit, Mont Ventoux is worth a visit no matter how you get there.

Both the *Gorges de la Nesque* and *Mont Ventoux* are major challenges to any serious cyclist and regularly feature in the *Tour de France,* which comes through or near the village every few years. By the time they reach the village most cyclists are hot and invariably they pause to fill their water bottles from the fountain and to dunk various over heated portions of their anatomies in the basin in order to take full advantage of its cooling potential. This Saturday had witnessed plenty of dunking.

The presence of a horse fair in the next village had brought a lone rider on horseback to our village to promote the afternoon's events and he spent a large portion of the morning giving free rides to the village children. Starting at the fountain, he loaded one child at a time into the saddle and then rode them round the village, returning each time to the fountain for the next child. Understandably, this gave rise to great excitement and drew crowds of eager children, overheating the poor horse. But the fountain was there, and after completing each circuit the horse was able to take a welcome drink from the basin – curling his lips with delight, sinking his muzzle into the cool water, lifting his head and enjoying the water sluicing away the dust – before setting off for the next circuit.

We have a number of colourful characters in the village, most of whom seem to have regular routines which involve walking around the centre of the village, meeting their friends for a chat and invariably ending up at the café across the road for a beer or a pastis in the morning, or under a tree in the square watching a game of boules in the afternoon. I mentioned Luc Travert earlier when I was writing about our summer concerts and Luc has dog, a huge, shaggy hound, which trots at his master's heels in all weathers. In the summer his tongue, the dog's that is, lolls out of his mouth and he seems to find each step more wearying than the last, much like his master, until he reaches the fountain where, with one last super-dog effort, he heaves himself over the edge of the basin and submerges with just his snout above water. After a couple of attempts at snorkelling the dog, suitably refreshed, leaps out and shakes himself dry before loping off to join his beloved master at the café, where at last he finds some shade beneath a table. And yes, this Saturday had been no different from any other day. The dog had made his customary visit to the fountain and had taken his daily bath earlier in the morning.

With so much interesting open country surrounding it, the village attracts a large number of visiting walkers. The serious hikers come with maps in plastic wallets, compasses and back packs stuffed with supplies against every contingency. Others, the amateurs, just arrive in their car, tumble out leaving it parked in the square, and set off. The idea of a walk in the country is an attractive one, but it needs to be put into context. Visitors from abroad or from the more northerly parts of France are not always aware of the speed with which the temperature rises in the mornings, and most return considerably bedraggled within an hour or so, having changed their mind about the joys of country life. They make a bee-line for the fountain, rinse their faces under the water spouts and then sit on the edge of the basin cooling their feet in the shady depths of the water.

Had the man in the car been sitting on our bench all morning, we were left wondering whether he would have been so eager to use the fountain's basin for his dental hygiene.

Oh, and something else which causes us some amusement is the notice pasted to the back of the fountain which reads 'This water is not fit for drinking'.

24

A question of taste – food and wine

By the time we arrived in Provence we had already acquired a taste for red wine. Over the years we had visited Bordeaux and had explored the vineyards of St Emillion, we had grown to like the wines from Corbières and the South West; we had worked our way across the Loire Valley and had drunk our way down the Rhone, from Beaujolais to the Mediterranean. Lest it sound like we are alcoholics I should mention that it took us twenty-five years to achieve this and in the process we had also discovered quite a lot of white, rosé and sparkling wines.

Living in Provence you cannot avoid the vine. Every scrap of ground is planted - even the plot of ground across the road from our house is planted with vines. The French take wine very seriously. I don't mean in the way that the English TV pundits do. Rather, the French expect to enjoy the wine that they drink and if it doesn't meet with their approval they open another bottle. We were at dinner with friends and there were three or four bottles of wine on the table and our host sampled them. He was not satisfied and went out to his cellar and came back with half a dozen more which he opened to find one that he thought was worthy of our consumption. Needless to say, by the end of the meal we had emptied the others as well.

When we first came to Provence every village had its own co-operative and most growers sent their grapes there for vinification. Nowadays there are many more small independent wine makers who have contracted out of the co-operatives in order to control the making of their own wine. In order to offset this, the standards of the co-operatives have risen steadily so that they are becoming more critical of the grapes they accept. The one good thing about having a co-operative in the village is that we can walk up and fill our cubi, a five litre plastic container, for the equivalent of 1.43€ per bottle - £1.05 in English currency – and that is for a quality wine, not merely 'vin de table' which costs considerably less.

The typical Côte de Ventoux is a spicy wine, strong in alcohol, with a rich fruity taste and a long, peppery finish. At its best, from Chateauneuf du Papes, or from Vacqueras or Gigondas it can stand comparison with any French wine. Every vintner we have visited has been more than ready to show us round his cellar and to provide us with plentiful samples – not just a sip, but a half glass of at least three of four different vintages. After a few such sessions we now ration ourselves to visiting only one vineyard on each occasion!

We would have been happy if the wine was all we found to enjoy, but there is so much more. The year starts with asparagus, fresh cut from the fields, purple, white or green, and delicious with hollandaise sauce. We have barely licked our lips when we have to begin on strawberries from Carpentras, with cherries following close on their heels. Most evenings in May and June we take a walk after dinner, finishing up in the cherry orchard at the foot of our garden. Untended for years – the owner died and his children have done nothing with the orchard – the trees are laden with fruit. And I can tell you that, picked from the tree and popped into your mouth, they are magnificent.

Melons from Cavaillon come next, and are taken very seriously. We stopped one afternoon on our way home and went into a roadside grower's yard.

'When did you want to eat it?' she asked us.

We replied for dinner but, since her offer was for three, she suggested that we take three and she carefully selected them at different stages of ripeness for us so that we could enjoy each one at its peak of perfection on successive days. In Provence, melons are not eaten chilled from the fridge, but are eaten fresh and sun-warmed so that their fragrance fills your nostrils and assails your taste buds before the fruit reaches your tongue. I must admit that a whole half, de-seeded and filled with Crème de Cassis is one of my favourite ways of eating melon. In passing I should tell you that we have been busy making jam from the strawberries and the cherries and also from fresh apricots picked from the local orchards. As the summer progresses we begin eating peaches, in the same sun-warmed way as we enjoy melon.

The olive has had a sudden lease of new life since we have all started eating sensibly, but olive trees, like vines, have been grown in Provence since Roman times. I don't want to enter into the argument about where you can buy the best olive oil, but we are content to buy our oil from a local mill. Every grocer has vats of olives where you ladle out what you want, and we were fascinated to note that they also provide little dishes for your olive pits – they would not dream of expecting you to buy without sampling first.

Having enjoyed olives, we became addicted to another Provençal delight – tapenade. This is a paste made from ground olives with various additions for flavour. That and brandande, a paste made from salted cod, spread thickly on crusty baguette is an aperitif without equal, particularly if consumed with a chilled rosé of the region.

No account of Provence would be complete without mention of Fougasse. This regional speciality is a flat bread, much like a thick pizza base, and is often flavoured with cheese or with lardons, crisp pieces of bacon. It can be oily, but is delicious and its characteristic shape is as delightful to the eye as its flavour is to the pallet.

Garlic is grown, and eaten, in quantity and is used freely in local cuisine. Its flavour, supported by herbs and tomatoes, forms the basis for most dishes. On our travels we had often bought Herbs de Provence and now that we are living here we have no problem finding them since they grow in our own garden. Sun scorched rosemary scents the air down our drive and thyme, trodden under foot, releases its oily fragrance. The climate is ideal for herbs and instead of the lush, flavourless growth in cooler, wetter climates, the growth is short and the flavour intense. The granite hillsides are clothed in herbs, and their scent mingles with the pine and lavender.

Sault, the next town from Villes sur Auzon, is famed for its lavender fields which turn its hillsides purple. You smell it before you see it, and the air is thick with its heady fragrance. The bees adore it and their honey is a local speciality. Honey is also one of the main ingredients of nougat, the other being almonds. Almond trees grow as freely as olive trees and green almonds are considered a delicacy. There is an almond tree on the corner of the orchard field at the end of our garden and one lady from the village regularly walks her dog past so that she can gather the fallen almonds, which she crushes open with a couple of stones. The first time we saw her sitting in the middle of the road, pounding away, we thought that she might have been 'slightly eccentric', but our strange looks did nothing to put her off.

There are several nougat makers in the region. One of the most famous is the family firm of Charles Boyer who have been making nougat for over a hundred years. Another nougat maker can be found in the tiny, nearby village of St. Didier, and this one is a particular delight because their factory is open to visitors and you can watch the process from start to finish through glass windows from their viewing gallery. You can then go into a special room where they roll and cut the nougat, giving you the trimmings for your instant gratification. French nougat, bought fresh from the maker, is soft, scented and wholly irresistible!

While we are talking about sweets, Carpentras, which we mentioned earlier as a centre for early strawberries, is also famous for its berlingots. These small, hardboiled fruit flavoured sweets are still made in the local shops as well as in the larger commercial factories.

No mention of food in Provence would be complete without mentioning the 13 desserts, a local Christmas favourite. Rooted in the Christian tradition, the thirteen desserts represent Christ and the twelve disciples. Although it doesn't have an exact prescription, there are usually certain elements that reflect local produce. The Marseille tradition has raisins, dried figs, almonds and nuts, candied plums, pears, apples and citrus fruit, quince jam, white and black nougat, yellow melon and fougasse. The dried fruits are called 'beggars' since their colours resemble those of the beggar monks, - Carmelites, Dominicans, Benedictines and Capuchins. A nut or an almond pricked into a fig is called Capuchin nougat. Oranges are a sign of personal wealth.

I could go on at length, but just writing about food and drink has made me hungry and thirsty …

25

To buy a fat pig

Visitors to France are always recommended to make their way to the local markets. They are a 'not-to-be-missed' feature of village life, the guidebooks tell us, a jewel in the crown of rural French life. The market in our village is tiny, usually no more than three stalls, although occasionally there is a fourth stall which sells clothes – not the fashionable but the 'shapeless and tasteless' variety so beloved by many of our elderly villagers. The proprietor sets out his racks and rails, erects a changing cabin, which looks suspiciously like a camping toilet tent, and does a brisk trade. The fruit and vegetable stall invitingly spreads over several tables in the full sun, and is there every week at first light when all sensible French housewives do their shopping and when the produce is crisp and inviting. By the time the tourists arrive not only has the best produce long since gone but the remains are tired, drooping and wrinkled.

The meat and fish stalls serve a steady trickle of customers throughout the morning. Cocooned in the cool air behind their refrigerated counters, they seem to be in no great hurry to serve and they have the time to exchange gossip with all their customers. Periodically another lorry arrives. Its arrival is advertised in advance and we receive thick colour brochures in our mail boxes, crammed with essential gadgets without which we wonder how we could exist. Supersonic anti-mole spikes vie for place amongst plastic frogs that croak every time someone passes them, and spanners of all sizes jostle for a place beside screwdriver kits with so many bits that I wonder how one ever finds the exact piece. There is always a queue at this stall – although only half the waiting crowd is eagerly purchasing gadgets, the other half is returning the items previously bought there and which no longer work.

Were that the sum total of our market experience then there would be little to become unduly excited about but there is more, much more. Nearly every village, large and small, has a market at least once a week, and some boast two markets every week. Large towns may have daily commercial markets. Visiting the market in a neighbouring village is an experience not to be missed.

There are two reasons why I like visiting markets. Apart from the obvious purchasing of goods, they provide an ideal place to pursue one of my favourite hobbies – people-watching. Bédoin market is an excellent place to indulge this pastime since it is one of the largest local markets and sprawls through the centre of the village, spilling into the side streets. We have been to this market in all the seasons of the year. Be the weather hot or cold, wet or dry, windy or calm, there is always something to see – it has never let us down.

It is true that we do buy produce – the cheese and local breads are often distinctive, and there is always a sausage stall where you can choose from a huge range of different flavours. Tasting is an important part of the purchase. In summer, if you start with the fruit and vegetables, there is usually some melon sliced up to try and then, moving on, there is often bread, invariably cheese, always sausage and olives and, more often than not, wine. Frequently we omit breakfast before coming to this market and, having sampled the goods on offer, we retreat to the café for a coffee which, sadly, we have to buy.

Besides food, there are other tempting goods on offer. There are stalls which sell the traditional Provençal materials at good prices and the 'seconds' from a local pottery are worth a moment or two of careful scrutiny. There are spice stalls whose fragrance draws you close, and stalls selling lavender where the scented oil hangs heavy in the air. You can buy all manner of hardware items and second hand books, tapes and CDs of all descriptions. Clothes and shoes, chairs and tables, sewing machines and water pumps – you can find most things if you look. Even so these are not the chief attractions. What makes the market really worth visiting is 'people-watching'.

In the summer the market will be packed with people from all over the world. You will stand shoulder to shoulder with a group of Chinese on one side of you whilst Dutch and Germans, Belgians and Danish, let alone the British and the French pass on the other ... the mix is amazing. At one moment you will be trying to disentangle Russian in one ear whilst your other is bombarded with some typically loud Australian homily.

Summer market walking is a hazardous pastime, and although you have to be prepared to sacrifice nearly every part of your person, it is the feet and the ribs that seem to suffer most. Our feet we expect to be crushed from time to time, but our ribs have had to learn the hard way that wicker baskets are indispensable in a market crowd. The safest way to 'people-watch' is to join the old men in the pavement café in the middle of the market. There you have some protection from being trampled and you have a grandstand view of the passing throng.

On our visit last week, we were particularly impressed by a very tall German father who was firmly strapped into his baby support frame. No simple sling this but a fully engineered, tensile aluminium, articulated frame, fitted to his shoulders and equipped with pneumatic shock absorbers so that the child would not be unduly bounced and ensuring that the poor father supporting his child would not be excessively bruised – advanced decoupling of a high standard. In most circumstances this would have been ideal – the child was elevated above his father's head with an uninterrupted panoramic view, riding in his cushioned cubicle

144

with little or no disturbance, somewhat like an Indian Rajah in a howdah on the back of an elephant.

However, owing to the height of his father, a good two metres we estimated, and the perennial need for shade that resulted in nearly every stall having a variety of awnings and umbrellas, the reality was not totally satisfactory. The man was striding through the market, scarcely pausing to look at the stalls less he disturb his young son, his wife walking confidently just in front, clearing a path lest her husband and child be jostled by the pressing crowds. But what neither of them saw was the poor child's head striking every awning and bumping against each umbrella. No matter how hard the poor child tried to dodge them his father's height ensured a perfect trajectory, and the efficiency of the suspension ensured that the father remained blissfully oblivious to the desperate movements of the little boy.

Odd fragments of conversation that drift out of the crowd, or are overheard as people pass by, can be both challenging as well as entertaining. I would love to know what one English couple were talking about when I caught the following fragment, 'Tell me, dear, if you see a woodpecker ...' or again, what were these two talking about 'I'm sure the goat doesn't mind!'

In a small town a little further away there is a huge flea market. Every Sunday morning the roads are jammed and cars, trailers and trucks are shunted into every available space as the masses invade in search of a bargain. It is one of the largest flea markets in France and here you will find stalls threaded along both banks of the river and through the whole town, selling everything you can imagine. Its speciality lies in the range of antique materials and 'collectables' that it offers in addition to the usual market goods. In the summer you can buy from gondolas which ply their wares up and down the river, adding a touch of Italian colour.

It is one of the most attractive markets, its ambience helped by shady trees and quaint, narrow, old streets where the stalls are set against timeless and utterly charming small town houses. Where else, we wondered, would you be able to buy English currency? We were fascinated by a stall selling current two pence pieces for the equivalent of £2.50 each. We hovered trying to see what business was like but it was too busy to stay still for long – although we were sorely tempted to set up a stall with the remains of our English small change.

As we have visited the local markets we have grown used to seeing the same stall keepers and hearing the same music. There is usually a portable fair ground organ at the larger markets with a large repertoire of favourites old and new, and there are often musical groups from Eastern Europe, some with gypsy violins, balalaikas and even one with a cimbalom. On some occasions our ears are tempted by the ethereal, haunting sound of pan-pipes and our eyes are drawn to the brightly colourful South American costumes. We have heard African musicians, a gospel choir and several jazz groups.

The ones to avoid are usually young and scruffy, cultivating a painfully thin and undernourished look, and who are in the early stages of the mastery of their chosen instrument. Frequently they have a guitar hung round their neck, and are connected to a portable amplifier, while some even run to a mouth organ on a frame which looks more like the handiwork of a malicious orthodontist than a musician. The musical diet on offer will range from page one of an appropriate *'How to play the ...'* book to a barely recognisable rending of a well known tune, and yes, I deliberately chose the word 'rending'. It always amazes me that they appear so hopeful whilst they are so hopeless.

Once the tourist season is over the markets contract a little, they slough off the inessentials and concentrate on what is necessary. The locals continue to buy the produce, and the offers are still there, but the crowds are smaller and it becomes possible to walk and talk in comfort. Sadly, the 'people-watching' becomes much less interesting – although once the Mistral returns it can enliven things in the most unpredictable ways.

26

The proper order of things

It is a commonly heard complaint that France is crippled by its bureaucracy. I have come to believe that this is a peculiarly non-French point of view since the French are nothing if not methodical.

There is a 'proper order' for most things, from the important issues of life to the trivia of daily existence. Take, for example, the saga of our telephone connection. When we first moved to France we thought it would be a good idea to have the telephone connected since there were already sockets in the house and a telephone line fixed to the outside of the house. This, we thought, would be a simple exercise and we set out to find the local *France Telecom* office in *Carpentras*.

Not knowing the geography of the town, it took us an inordinate amount of time to find their office. Every direction we were given took us to long, straight, one-way roads leading out of town. We then had to drive on to the next roundabout in order to return to town for another try. We repeated this exercise several times before we found a car park. We were not much more successful on foot and it took us another half an hour before we found the office. Needless to say, when we finally located *France Telecom* it had its own car park. At least having travelled so many of them by the end of that morning, we began to learn the layout of the roads – the 'proper order' of things.

The next discovery was that, like most businesses in France, the office closed at mid-day on the dot. We arrived ten minutes after they had closed and just as they were letting out their last customers. But at least we were able to find the office at our first attempt in the afternoon, now that we knew the 'proper order' of things.

Like many such offices, France Telecom operates a queuing system that was not immediately apparent. When we entered there appeared to be people walking about looking at the displays, assiduously studying new equipment or just sitting reading magazines, and there were no signs of queues, orderly or otherwise. The reality was much more subtle and after reporting to the reception desk our name was entered into their computer system and we had to wait until we were called. We were not immediately aware of the procedure, of the 'proper order' of things, and were not a little confused when, having explained our business, we were left to our own devices.

In due course, however, our name was called and we were given excellent service by an English speaking assistant who moved heaven and earth, or at least the internal bureaucracy of *France Telecom*, to put us on-line straight away. It proved complicated to identify our existing line, because we did not then know any of the names of our neighbours, and even an on-screen map of the location of our house didn't seem to make tracing the line any easier. We were given our new number and we bought a telephone, but we had to go home and await the arrival of an engineer to make the connection. When he came two days later it took him a matter of two minutes to look at the wire, trace it to a junction box and insert the bridging pin to make the connection. Quite simple, really, it was just a matter of following the correct procedures, the 'proper order' of things.

When we came to live permanently in France, we needed to move the telephone to our new house, which also had telephone points throughout the house and a visible telephone line running from our house via the house next door to a telephone pole. Wiser, and having learnt by our last experience, we visited *France Telecom* once again and were greeted by the same English speaking assistant who, as before, gave us excellent service and arranged for the transfer of our number, the disconnection of the old line and a visit by a technician to re-connect the new line. Highly pleased we left to await the technician's visit, scheduled for the following day.

He arrived, looked over the line and scaled his ladder to see if he could make the connection. All was not well – the line was dead, he told us. He tested the connection in our house and then went back to his ladder, leaning against the derelict house next door, and tested the connection there. No luck! He traced the line down the wall to the ground and probed behind the covering. Suddenly he leaped up and started to blow on his fingers.

'Bees,' he said. 'A wild bee's nest.'

Nothing deterred, he carried on and rang back to his head office for assistance. He was told that we would have to have a new line since they could no longer connect us via someone else's property – it was no longer considered the 'proper order' of procedure.

We had no choice but to agree although we were beginning to worry about the cost, having had some experience of BT. The next day we were visited by another technician and were impressed by his promptness. He surveyed the scene and told us what we would need, and then told us that we'd have to make a hole through the house wall through which he could pass the wire. Couldn't he do it, we asked? He looked at us aghast – he was a France Telecom engineer, not a *maçon*. He suggested that we do it ourselves.

'Just go up into the roof and knock a hole through!'

What could be easier? He had even told us the diameter of the hole we needed to make and also, he suggested, we should have some conduit to put the wire through. He promised to return the next afternoon. We rushed off and bought the conduit and a large masonry chisel to make the hole. Back home, and with considerable trepidation, we explored the inside of our roof.

Unlike English houses, property here is built with solid floors and ceilings. Quite understandable on the ground floor and even on the first floor since all our floors are tiled, but we had not expected the upstairs ceiling to be solid concrete. This gave us some confidence moving about in the roof, but it did mean that we had to work very hard boring a hole through the ceiling to pass the new wire down into my study.

Having paid due attention to the 'proper order' of things we awaited the arrival of the technician the following afternoon. He came immediately after lunch, scaled his ladder and ran in the new line from the telephone pole in the road to our house. We showed him the conduit and his face fell.

'Where is the pull wire?' he asked.

It seems that conduit is supplied with or without a threaded wire to pull the cables through, and we had bought conduit without the pull wire. We were informed that he couldn't use this but he offered to make the connection if we managed to thread the wire through for him! We were beginning to become a little jaundiced by then but, having got this far, we weren't prepared to give in that easily so we unrolled the conduit in the roof and managed to thread the new cable without any great difficulty. Now everything was in the 'proper order' the technician was able to make the connections and in a matter of minutes he put in two new outlets exactly where we wanted them and was on his way. Incidentally, there was no charge for the work.

We had been surprised that we had needed to make a separate hole for the entry of the telephone line in the first place since it is immediately next to four open air bricks which ventilate the roof space and the telephone line could easily have passed through one of them – the actual wire is less than five millimetres thick and the air bricks have holes of a much large diameter. And then again, we wondered why we had to bore a twenty-two millimetre hole for the cable, but then, I suppose there is a 'proper order'.

There is a postscript to this tale. A year later we were working outside when we became increasingly aware of insects flying around the roof and eventually going in and out of the telephone line hole. It had not been part of the technician's role to fill the hole and so it had remained partially open making a perfect landing place for bees and wasps. Except that the wasps we were watching looked rather large. We were due to have the house walls re-surfaced and the builder came to offload the scaffolding. We pointed out the insect activity to him, and he told us that they were not wasps but hornets, and that we should call the fire brigade who dealt with such things. We were happy to do just that and *les pompiers* arrived in the early evening. Apparently, in the 'proper order' of things, it is one of their jobs to deal with wasp nests.

We were impressed by the two men who came and by the speed with which they investigated the probable nest in the roof. When they came down they said that we had two small wasp nests, not hornet's nests, and that they would remove them. It is just as well we had called them early, they told us, because the nests can become very large and within a month could have become bigger than a football. They had even dealt with hornet nests that had been too big to remove through ordinary doors – by now the gestures were becoming more and more expansive, and we were reminded that fishing is the largest sport in France. Certainly these two were well into fishermen's yarns we thought watching their arm gestures.

Outside, in front of the garage, the elder fireman began to remove his clothes, which caused Christine to raise her eyebrows and then lower her eyes, and climbed into his protective all-in-one suit which was a masterly garment with built in rubber gloves, a crash helmet and face net all in thick, dark blue cotton. Unfortunately he was a large fireman and the suit seemed surprisingly small. The two of them struggled for a while but when the zip stuck, they finally gave up and tried to remove the suit – which proved even more difficult than putting it on. After a quick inspection, they then repeated the process but with the suit the other way round and all went well – the 'proper order' of things...

Suited, with his huge leather boots on, his visor closed, armed with his pump spray and looking not unlike Neil Armstrong – he even had a touch of the 'moon walk' about him – the fireman re-entered the house. The trap door into our roof space is in the tiny upstairs utility room and has a very narrow hatch. Needless to say the suited fireman couldn't pass through and so had to remove his sprayer, which then had to be twisted and turned to pass it through the hatch. A little later they were both back outside, mission accomplished.

At this point we thought it helpful to offer iced water since the roof had been baking all the afternoon, and the temperature on our terrace had reached 49°C. Suitably refreshed they inspected the hole through which the wasps had been going in and out. They were concerned to see that the flights continued, seemingly undiminished, and so they fetched the large ladder from their tender and climbed up to have a look at the hole from the outside taking the spray and squirting the hole from the outside for good measure. Still the hornets came, flying in and out and looking to our eyes very cross – the firemen returned to ground rather promptly.

A further inspection of the nests in the roof resulted in their asking for a hammer and chisel and they removed part of the block through which the cable ran. They came down hastily after this and suited up again. This time they had found a large hornet's nest and further treatment was needed. Shortly after, bits of nest started coming through the air brick as they removed the nest which the hornets had craftily built into the void in the concrete block. This time the flights ceased and all seemed to be quiet at last – if it hadn't been the eastern side of the house I would have said 'everything was quiet on the western front' – anyway, the 'proper order' had been restored. It seemed that the wasps – no real danger – used the air brick for their entrance but the hornets – potentially very dangerous – had used the telephone cable access which is why they had not initially been seen from the inside. Even the insect world, it seems, observes the 'proper order' of things.

27

Quiet thoughts

By day our village is noisy and busy with people. Throughout the summer tourists traipse through and children race their bikes round the square, in and out of the elderly men playing boules. It can be just as busy, and just as noisy, at night but on occasion calm descends.

They started working on the lights round the village in the spring, and have just finished the new installations. The old lights in the square were on tall metal posts, efficient but ugly, and there was always the possibility that the poles could find themselves in the way of an inebriated late-night car. Now the poles have gone and the old efficient lights which were designed to flood light the square for late night boules have been removed. In their place we have much more tasteful lantern-style fittings all round the perimeter of the square, fixed to the house walls, along passageways and under the old arched portal. The new lights don't provide such a strong light but they wash the square with a more sophisticated glow, and are probably just as efficient as the former ones. The places where the poles once stood are now empty and we await developments, debating with ourselves as to whether the powers that be will plant trees or just flatten the mounds. We suspect that there are more elaborate plans afoot since the square is now scarred by a few roughly filled in trenches where the new electricity cables have been laid. Perhaps we will soon have proper boules pitches and marked out parking with the whole resurfaced and levelled.

The cosmetic glow from the new lights is intriguing since at night it invests crumbling walls, broken stonework, flaking paint and rotting wood with a distinctly charming, old-world chic. The parts of the village that had seemed derelict by day suddenly become endowed with new life – that which was ugly is transformed into charming, dirty becomes quaint and falling down transmogrifies into artistic.

We were at a concert last evening, sitting in the deep shade of the plane trees listening to a lady singing to the accompaniment of a guitar. Carried by the sound of her voice my thoughts were drifting out of control. I guess by now you'll know that there was nothing unusual about that. The first thing that occupied my attention was the cloud of mosquitoes hovering over the audience. I could almost hear them rubbing their hands with glee, 'rich pickings tonight' they were buzzing to each other. Periodically throughout the next hour I was reminded of their presence and forced to join my neighbours in a few swift smacks and sharp brushings of exposed parts of my person, particularly my bald head since it seemed that the mosquitoes had taken a liking to skating.

Then there was the distinctive sound of the singer's voice, the cadences of the French language are so different from English. She sang effortlessly, the sound a subtle blend of speech and vocalising, an intimate whisper alternating with a more assertive line, the tone suddenly harsh and then tender. The audience knew most of the songs and there was a resonance hanging in the air as they hummed along, folk songs rubbed shoulders with offerings from Asnavour, Distel and Piaff.

Her accompanist was playing on a guitar made in our village. Every time we walk to the doctor's we pass the luthier's house and look into the downstairs windows of his workshop which is hung with the tools of his trade, moulds and templates, gauges and callipers, gouges and saws. Partly finished tables of instruments rest alongside finger-boards emerging from pieces of wood, one time a pot of glue will be set to warm and on another the scent of polish will hang in the air. Now, listening to the sounds drawn from the instrument, I marvel at the skills that have gone into the making of this ephemeral moment, and I pause to consider if the person who planted the tree, or the woodcutter, imagined this moment.

Handicapped by my lack of understanding, the subtlety of the words passes me by and in the gathering darkness my eye is drawn to the houses behind the performers. We are in a corner of the village, on the outside of the inner 'circle', and are gathered between houses and the old fountain on a triangle of ground that is normally used by the residents for parking. Tonight the road has been closed and barriers erected guaranteeing us some relief from cars and space to relax. The houses are jumbled together – a long row turns at the left of my vision, veering to my right and making the backdrop for the musicians. There is a narrow opening at the right hand side and we can see houses sneaking away at the end of this row of three houses. The other side, on my right, is made up of another group which seem to have staggered into the space. Higgledy-piggledy they are squashed in; some thin some wide, some tall and one short. They continue along the side in an irregular row, disappearing behind me as the road bends towards the luthier's house on the corner. Immediately behind me the fountain is set in a cobbled patch and plays along with the musicians, splashing a counterpoint to their cantus firmus, whilst on my left the road follows the inner circle of houses that form the core of the village.

The three houses behind the singer are old. Not as old, certainly, as the original village houses on my left, but dating from the seventeenth or eighteenth century. How many times have they been occupied and by whom? How many times have they been restored, renovated, and converted? Two are presently empty, run down and in need of repair. The stones are partially exposed, the rendering has fallen off in places and there are dangerous bulges in the walls. The wood of the window frames is rotten with not a vestige of paint left after many years of sun, wind and rain. The shutters are closed, bare wood weathered to a mellow grey, rust streaking down from the hinges strapped to their fronts. And yet there are noble proportions to the houses, the stone casements for the windows suggest once proud builders, people with an eye for balance, and the mouldings suggest that they were seeking a touch of elegance beyond the ordinary.

The new village lights are represented here, a sleek new black lantern fixed to the centre house, its downcast rays picking out the chiaroscuro of the stone wall. The warm glow of the light picks out the deep ochre stains running in swirls across the front of the house and the colder white patches of stone are thrown into relief. A creeper has started to spread its tendrils from the occupied house next door, shyly seeking new finger holds and promising in return to provide dignified cover for the embarrassed stones. The fronts of the houses look like a Pollock masterpiece, traces of wire for the telephone, cables for the street lights and power for the houses criss-cross each other, separating the patches of colour and the distressed stonework, running on to the neatly rendered exterior of the last house in the row.

Across the passageway the next house has been restored and newly painted. Dark green shutters are closed in the deep red ochre of the façade – new owners here, and new pride for the house. A shining brass knocker awaits the guests and invites the new owner to open the door and I wonder if it also stirs the shadows of the house's distant past. The next house has its curtains apart and we can glimpse an ancient bread oven in the kitchen. No longer functional, it has become a smart place for the micro-wave; 'instant' Chinese from the freezer has replaced the rich aroma of freshly baked bread.

We always refer to the fountain as the 'old' fountain but a moment's thought leads me to suspect that it must once have been the 'new' fountain. When the village was fortified, and its residents sheltered and contained by the surrounding wall, there would have been no cause for a fountain outside the village. In hostile times what use would that have been but to help make the attacker more comfortable? We know from local history that the village fountains were an integral part of daily life providing water not only for the villagers' consumption but for washing, for the growing of food and for the washing of ochre. Water has been at the centre of village life for centuries and remains just as important today. Although no longer consumed by the villagers since it has been certified as 'unfit for drinking' the fountain continues to refresh by its sound and like the other fountains in the village is still used by some for their washing, by others, including us, for cleaning our floors and the water still finds its way into gardens.

We leave quietly at the end of the first half, nursing our bites. Footsteps echo behind us and a child's voice is singing a catchy phrase from one of the songs, the mother joins in. We are intrigued and slow our pace hoping that they will pass us but they seem to have slowed to match our pace, fuelling our curiosity. We pause at the corner, perhaps now they will go past. I bend to tidy my shoelace and at last they move by. A little girl, scarcely taller than my knee, is singing and swinging on her mother's hand. The son walks more soberly with his father as befits the growing maturity of five years. My last thought before turning in at our gate, is that these children have had an experience that they may well remember for the rest of their lives. What riches they will have to draw upon.

28

Bastille Day, again

The wheel has turned, the calendar has completed its cycle and it is once more time to celebrate another revolution. The fourteenth of July has come again. How quickly the past year has gone!

It was much like last year, at first there were no notices to be seen and then, about a week ago, they were posted and we began to anticipate the delights to come. The evening of the fourteenth began much like it had done last year, at about 21.00. But this year, instead of the ceremonial firing of the cannon, three rockets were sent up outside the *Mairie*. They not only exploded with showers of glittering stars but also with ear shattering noise. The pigeons, already settled in the dark of the tree branches, launched themselves shrieking and squawking their protest as the first explosion echoed over the village only to be set off again by the second and then the third. As peace and quiet settled back down around us, and not a few feathers, the music from the funfair in *La Place* resumed its thump and the little children began to pester their parents to light their lanterns.

The band arrived and gave its customary stirring rendition of *La Marseillaise*. The villagers seemed to have made little progress in learning the words of *La Marseillaise* and I was still able to join in - De-de-de Dah Dah Dum… After this, everything seemed to go quiet and there was a space where nobody seemed to do anything, and so we all waited patiently, the children swinging their lanterns and the adults trying to restrain them. At last the band moved off and we all followed along the main road, lit once again by Roman Candles, and we choked on the acrid smoke hanging under the trees.

This year's specialities were two set-piece firework displays, one in front of the church and the other half way round at the *Grand Portail* where part of the display was against the old gateway and part was on the opposite side of the road on the old fountain.

The first, at the church, began with a very noisy and unexpected set of fire crackers that made us all step back quickly from the roped off area. These were followed by 'fountains and candles' in bright colours, first at one side of the huge doors and then on the other. There were large fountains on the church steps as well, and the whole scene was painfully colourful. Just as our eyes had started to adjust to their brilliance the fountains began to fade and rockets took over, whizzing noisily up into the dark sky. Multi-coloured and full of *stars*, the rockets were very good although, because of the overhanging trees, we didn't see much of them. We saw them rise, heard the bangs and saw the falling showers of stars. We were all crowded round in the road, trying to shelter from the 'fallout' but 'ooh-ing' and 'ah-ing' appropriately. As the rockets came to an end a 'waterfall' which had been cunningly hidden over the arch of the church doors began to cascade its silver-bright showers and once more we clapped to show our appreciation. The whole had been electronically triggered and had gone off without a hitch.

Tradition dictated that there was a bonfire in the middle of the road outside the church and an informal farandole-like chain grew out of the crowd and danced around it whilst a few brave people leaped over the flames. Wonderful pagan rites just outside the church! We also had three 'street entertainers', a man and a lady on high stilts and a juggler. The juggler worked very hard, but kept dropping his balls, clubs or whatever. We didn't understand what the stilt-people were trying to do. The girl kept holding out a scarf, and it looked like she was trying to shake crumbs off a tablecloth, whilst the man just walked and hopped about. We don't think anyone else knew what they were up to, either, but it made a change and gave us something else to talk about.

The procession moved on and came to its next stop against the *Grand Portail* where there was another fireworks display. Like the one at the church it began with a fire-cracker set and was followed by similar displays. The set piece this time was a huge Catherine Wheel which span at an amazing speed for what seemed like ages before it finally faded. A few more huge bangs and we were on our way once more, heading for *La Place* where the band entertained us for a while as we waited for the 'striptease'.

You will remember that last year we had *'Les Body Boy'* and this year, since we are a democracy, we were promised *'Le strip-tease'*. When the band finished, the disco took over and there was dancing as we all waited and the juggler did another set, with about as much success as the previous time, and the stilt walkers continued...to walk...

The strip-tease had a great deal of tease, and very little strip, with three girls clad in glittery bikinis gyrating various parts of their anatomies for our approval – although in their second set one did come on stage in a dress and gloves...and stripped back down to her bikini... All in the best possible taste and to the considerable disappointment of the red blooded males. We returned home at half past midnight.

The celebrations continued throughout the week and there were various competitions, meals, dances and events as well as the fun-fair. We walked back down on the last night when an informal dance was to take place in *La Place*. It had been a long week and the village was tired, the dancing was minimal and most people were seated at the tables near the buvette. That's not to say that the event was a failure – far from it –

the band was superb. We counted about thirteen musicians and three dancers.

They were set up on a tiered platform which was draped in black and had glitter curtains shimmering in the breeze from electric fans beneath them, which picked up the colours from the spotlights. A vocalist held centre-stage and as he sang the dancers provided the vocal backing as well as dancing. After each number they filtered off at the back, and there was either a change of vocalist or an instrumental number. The transition was very slick and professional and moved into the next number with the dancers back in new costumes and a change of mood. We took in Rock 'n Roll, Twenties Flappers, Latin American, Blues, Jazz, and even a number with Nuns who were 'none' too well behaved. Periodically an accordion player took over and gave the musicians a rest. We were very impressed by him and were amazed at the speed with which his fingers found their way over the button keyboard.

As before, the whole event was relaxed and there was no sign of unease. Old couples sat at the tables, young parents walked with the little children in their pushchairs, teenagers mixed with toddlers, campers came and visitors joined the residents, everyone was welcome and found a place. Different styles of dancing made room for each other, an elderly couple doing a 'smooch' in the old-fashioned way steered themselves round a young man flinging his partner over his shoulders in the best rock 'n roll style and moved in and out of 'singles' just jigging about because it seemed like a good thing to do. There was a little girl who stationed herself in the centre of the dancing area. She must have been about five and she watched each and every dance on the stage and then within a few bars she had the routine memorised and was imitating the professionals so well that she was a delight to watch. She had such concentration and made so much effort, the rhythm seemed to come from within her. She was very good.

162

The music pressed on without a break. It was there to listen to, for dancing, to watch or just as a pleasant background. No hassle, no charge and a wonderful end to a busy week.

29

Moving on

We've been on holiday. Well, almost. We went to Toulouse to look at an organ only to find that the studio was closed for a week. Rather than go home, we decided to visit some of our old haunts in the Vendée.

La Timonerie
September, 2003

Dear Mum and Dad,

Take a deep breath and read on slowly. No, it's not bad news and no, you're not about to have another grandchild! You know that we took a few days off last week to travel across to Toulouse and visit the organ shop there. Well, it was shut when we finally found it – closed for their annual week's holiday. It took us a while, and a lot of deep breaths and counting to significantly high numbers before we were calm enough to think what to do next. Finally, we decided that since Bendicks was snug in the cattery, we'd take a few more days off and visit some of our old haunts up country along the Atlantic coast.

We had a super journey up and found a place to stay just outside Niort with a restaurant opposite. Full of trepidation we drove towards Luçon, the nearest town which lies comfortably between Niort and the coast. It was much as we remembered it – you'd have recognised the gardens where we used to eat lunch – and apart from a small development in the centre it was delightfully familiar and welcoming. We drove on towards the coast and the little village where we used to caravan all those years ago when the children were small. Again, although you only came with us once, you'd have felt at home immediately. There were a few more houses on the outskirts where formerly there had been just building plots for sale, but the village centre was unchanged. As we crossed the road from the car park we walked past the estate agent's window and curiosity drew us to look at the houses and, well, one thing led to another, and we found ourselves inside.

Christine spun him a lovely tale about needing a larger house because I was going to buy an organ and our present house had too many neighbours, and how I would have to play it quietly. And then there was the garden, she wanted to grow more vegetables and terrain was so expensive where we lived and the cost of watering – I was almost in tears myself, albeit tears of mirth. The agent was charming and passed us on to his assistant who spoke English. Christine explained it all again with even more heart rending embellishments.

He told us he knew exactly what we wanted and went through to the back office, returning in a couple of moments with three folders in his hand. He enthused about all three properties telling us about the gardens and how each had a large room for the organ – we were impressed. But we were dumbfounded when he asked if we had time to look at them. If we had, he said, he'd take us right now.

Well, what could we do? We didn't want to tell him that we weren't really serious and there again, one of them sounded intriguing. We set off at break-neck speed through narrow, twisting country roads and visited the first two in record time. We didn't like either of them but were too polite to say so and instead we made well-bred and hopefully non-committal noises.

'Wait until you see the last one,' he said, 'I'm sure it will be just what you want and I'm certain that the owner will accept an offer.'

He indicated the sort of price he had in mind and we were certainly interested! Back through the same twisting roads, further towards the coast and out into the country. Certainly we wouldn't disturb the neighbours, we said. He turned off the deserted road into a little lane and at the end against the fields there was a low two-storey cottage. It looked a little like a fisherman's cottage we thought as we got out of the car and crossed over to the house. It had a single storey extension at each end, the furthest adjoining a huge two-storey barn. The house was empty, he explained since the owners were away. He showed us round.

There was a large entrance hall with stairs leading up at the rear, and to the right a large lounge with a kitchen area and two bedrooms opening off at the far end into the single storey extension. Upstairs he showed us a huge bedroom and an even larger space over the rest of the house which was floored but not completed. There was very little to do apart from adding wall linings. There were stone steps leading from a door down to the outside. Downstairs he took us through the other side of the hall to a huge and fully modernised bathroom with a separate toilet, a large shower and twin basins. Another door took us into a utility room with fridges, a washing machine and a double sink. There was a door out to the garden at the rear.

'But this is what I wanted you to see,' he said opening the barn door. 'It's been re-roofed and the walls are all in good condition. All it needs is a floor and then you could convert it into anything you wanted. It would make a super space for an organ!'

It was amazing. There were no uprights; the roof was modern, on rafters so the whole space was empty and two stories high. The barn was about 10m by 12m, big enough we quickly estimated to make about four rooms. Outside there was a good area of ground, surrounded by fields with the edges already planted to trees and there was a generous strip of ground on each side of the house. There was another house on the other side of the road behind a fringe of trees and a farm nearby with cattle sheds but, apart from these, the house was quite on its own. The sea, he told us, was about five kilometres away, across the fields.

We looked round again, more interested this time, and then made our way back to the village. We thanked him for his time and said that we'd like to think about all the houses we'd seen and would call back the following Monday.

The barn was such an amazing space and the price was so low that we could afford to have the alterations done for us. Suddenly we found ourselves tempted by the idea. And what a temptation! It took our breath away and even though we drove on towards the beach we didn't really notice the sea. Our eyes were already busy with the alterations to the barn, planting the garden... We were all for dashing back and making an offer straight away. But how could we?

When we moved to Provence it was with the full expectation that we would remain there for a long time and if anyone had suggested that within three years we would be on the move again we would have thought them mad. The best laid plans...

We had no thoughts of moving and were as surprised as you probably are to discover that we could contemplate such an idea so easily.

'What has happened?' we hear you asking.

We were busy asking ourselves the same question. Nothing! We love living in Provence and are settled and content, the weather really suits us and the sense of belonging to our village is stronger than any that we have known. And yet, we do find ourselves thinking if only we had a little more garden or a little more space in the bedroom – little things. And then there is the letting house. It has been a wonderful way of meeting different people, of sharing our delight in living here and yet it is expensive to maintain. The constant need to advertise and the vagaries of the tourist business make it a dubious investment and one which we have been forced to review after a quiet season. After all, as pensioners we must look to our income!

I think we were like 'ground' that is described as being 'ready for planting'. From a strange impulse a whole chain of events was carrying us along and we scarcely had time to think. Until we'd had our evening meal, that is, and then we sat on the bed and carefully went through all the things that had happened over the last few hours. We decided to sleep on it and see what our subconscious made of it all.

In the morning we were just as intrigued as we had been the night before and so we decided to visit the house on our way to the beach. We walked round it, took the external measurements and began to think seriously about what we could do with it. The actual house, although it was pleasant enough, wasn't really as good as the one where we are presently living but it would make a letting house if we converted the barn for our use.

Perhaps it was the challenge of converting it, or the promise of what it might offer, or even just the proximity of the sea, something was pulling us to consider this more carefully. We passed a lovely afternoon lying in the sun on the nearly deserted sands of the beach and talked on and on about it. We decided to come back on Monday and ask the agent if he would take us to look at it again. We felt sufficiently interested to take it seriously.

Back at the hotel again, we decided that if we really liked it we should go and visit some other properties in the surrounding areas, to see if it really was outstanding or if we were just being carried along on a wave of nostalgia. After all, we said, when we get back to Provence it'll all seem like a dream and we'll be so happy to be back that we'll know we were suffering from temporary insanity.

Our final visit on Monday confirmed what we had thought, and it did seem possible that we could make a good conversion of the barn and adapt the other end of the house for letting. We were sure that being so close to the sea we'd have no problem in letting it fully throughout the summer months. We drove off into the countryside determined to find out what else was on offer.

Our first experience was interesting. We found a castle! It was splendidly isolated in about seven acres of ground, set atop a little hill with spectacular views. But the price was too high, the owner extremely eccentric and on the whole we felt it was too draughty to make a snug home, although we could have done a lot with the garden. Other houses were poorly situated, or the outbuildings were in too poor a state of repair, or the houses needed too much renovation... There was an endless series of little problems. Another had superb open spaces downstairs but the bedrooms were hopeless, yet another had a lovely mezzanine lounge but the garden was too enclosed by trees... We found excuse after excuse. Nothing could quite compare with our barn – yes, we were beginning to think of it as 'our' barn!

Our last day took us into the country side about an hour away from La Rochelle, a little further inland than we wanted to be, but we felt that we should look at what was on offer here as well since it was still in the micro-climatic zone which should ensure mild winters and hot summers.

We visited an old Charantaise Longère, a long farm house. It was delightfully set in deep countryside, surrounded by fields and had a good collection of outbuildings, one of which had been restored and tidied. There was a small barn in need of work and a tall barn attached to the house which still had its original bread oven, complete with rakes and paddles. The owner had started work on the house but the modernisation had not been completed and it was variable in quality. The kitchen was in a long conservatory-like extension which ran the length of the back of the house. It was tempting but not as good as 'our' barn.

Our last house, the one we would visit before we bought 'our' barn we told ourselves, had to wait until after lunch because the owner was out and so we drove into the nearest village, which had a cattle market just finishing, and had a pleasant lunch of baguette sandwiches and I indulged myself with *une pression*, beer from the pump, the first beer I have ever bought myself!

Back in agent's car we made our way back towards the Longère we had visited earlier, but instead we went to a similar house about five hundred metres further along the road. It lay back from the road and we entered along a tree lined drive which had a neat stone wall along one side. We drove between a very large barn and the stone house and the agent pulled the car up on a sunny, gravel terrace in front of the house. It seemed very long and we had to turn our heads to take it all in. It was nothing special, we thought, but well-set in an established garden. It also had its original bread oven as well as ponds and another long, single storey barn which we were told was a former pigsty. There were two paddocks, one at the front and the other across the rear. We went in. The kitchen seemed dark after the bright sunlight and we were given a quick tour and shown the bathroom which opened off the kitchen and the boiler room with a loft room above. Back into the kitchen and through into the lounge.

We stopped in our tracks, struck dumb.

Why? What happened? Go on! We can hear you now. Well, we will. But … in our next letter —